Chasing the Light
THE CLOUD CULT STORY

Mark Allister

Foreword by Mark Wheat

University of Minnesota Press
Minneapolis · London

Interview excerpts from the film *No One Said It Would Be Easy* are reproduced by permission of John Paul Burgess.

Cloud Cult lyrics are reproduced by permission of Cloud Cult/Craig Minowa.

Photographs are reproduced by permission of Cloud Cult/Craig Minowa unless otherwise credited. Thanks to Jeff DuVernay, Cody York (http://www.cody yorkphotography.com), and Stacy Schwartz (http://www.stacyannschwartz .com) for contributing photographs to the book.

Published by the University of Minnesota Press
111 Third Avenue South, Suite 290
Minneapolis, MN 55401–2520
http://www.upress.umn.edu

Design and production by Mighty Media, Inc.
Interior and text design by Chris Long

Library of Congress Cataloging-in-Publication Data
Allister, Mark.
Chasing the light : the Cloud Cult story / Mark Allister ; foreword by Mark Wheat.
ISBN 978-0-8166-9653-6 (pb : alk. paper)
1. Cloud Cult (musical group). 2. Rock musicians—United States—Biography.
I. Title.
ML421.C59A45 2014
782.42166092'2—dc23
[B]
                                                      2014017603

Printed in the United States of America on acid-free paper made from 100% post-consumer recycled material

The University of Minnesota is an equal-opportunity educator and employer.

20 19 18 17 16 15 14   10 9 8 7 6 5 4 3 2 1

For Meredith Coole Allister, partner extraordinaire

When your life is finished burning down,
You'll be all that's left standing there.
You'll become a baby cumulus,
And fly up to the firmament.

No one gets to know the purpose,
We need to learn to live without knowing.
But all we are saying is
Step forward, step forward.

We can only see a small part of
Everything and nothing.
When you finally know you can't know,
Step forward, step forward.

—Cloud Cult, "Step Forward"

Contents

foreword

MARK WHEAT

When I heard Cloud Cult's first album *Who Killed Puck,* put together by Craig Minowa alone in 2001, I remember thinking that it was brilliant and beautiful but had no chance of being a success. I was lucky to be working at the University of Minnesota college station Radio K then, in the cynical world left after the 1990s. Within the music business the promise of the alternative revolution had turned crass and exploitative. Minowa seemed so open and vulnerable with a wonderful naïveté wrapped in interesting tunes expressed with such utter sincerity that I thought the business would eat him up and spit him out in no time. Since then, I have watched, both delighted and dumbfounded at every step of his success along the way, thinking, if he can keep going, so can I, however bizarre and soul-destroying dealing with this industry can be.

Cloud Cult has been an inspiration to me working at Radio K and Minneapolis Public Radio's The Current. In turn, according to Mark Allister's *Chasing the Light,* the band has been inspired by what we at small, nonprofit radio stations across the country have done for them. They are kindred spirits, and over the years I've been blessed by a handful of short significant meetings with them that all stuck with me. And judging by the testimonials in this book, Cloud Cult has done this with almost every single one of its fans.

Craig and Connie Minowa have been listening to The Current since we came on in 2005. They once sent an e-mail message while listening to me ring in the New Year: spending New Year's Eve with The Current had become their tradition. And something I said on *Musicheads,* a podcast hosted by colleague Bill DeVille, resonated so much with Craig that he made a creative decision based on it: forty-five minutes is a good length for an album. This used to be the average length in the days of vinyl purely because of the limitation of the medium. With CDs able to hold seventy minutes, most bands, including Cloud Cult, extended album length. All of the band's first five albums are over fifty minutes, two of them over an hour. But there's something organic that forty-five minutes produces that works for us; I'm not sure why. So in 2008 when *Feel Good Ghosts* came out, we had the band on our stage at South by Southwest. I told Minowa how tight the album was at thirty-nine minutes long, that he had focused his work better than ever. He admitted that he had taken my opinion seriously and decided to keep it short.

The video from a 2007 Current session in which Cloud Cult performs "Pretty Voice" is one of the most watched we have ever had, with more than 850,000 views. Watch another video on You-Tube of the band from that SXSW show in Austin, doing "No One Said It Would Be Easy." Minowa has one bare foot and one socked foot. Seeing him dance between the cords on the floor of our studio when they came in to do their first session with us made me feel more closely connected to this artist I had admired for years from a distance. I have always tried to deejay in my socks—it's a comfort thing that was difficult only at Minneapolis's First Avenue because of the nastiness of the floor! As soon as I get to work at Minnesota Public Radio, I put my slipper socks on: it's my way of feeling at home, grounding myself. Few musicians seem to share this habit, but Minowa does, even on First Avenue's stage.

I witnessed that at The Current's eighth birthday in January 2013. Having the fortune to watch the band from the First Avenue owners' box was a highlight of my career. Only owner Dayna Frank could see the tears streaming down my face, and I think she understood. That night Cloud Cult was putting one of its maxims into practice: *be here now,* in the present moment. What they were playing was not just another set of songs; it was special, for them and for us as the audience. Cloud Cult celebrated the station by playing the songs that they connected with The Current, singles we had played and songs our audience had discovered. Minowa told several stories explaining how important the connection to radio is for the band. What a perfect way to celebrate what we have going for us here in Minnesota, too: a public radio station supported by its audience that inspires local-artist, self-propelled bands like Cloud Cult who are making a living from their art. No other band better represents that local pride of place, even though they moved to a farm in Wisconsin!

I approach this book as more than just a deejay or critic who has admired them in the past. This is a personal connection for me that I cherish and really could only share with you in this foreword for Mark's book. After reading the book, you'll understand the importance of radio to Minowa and the band's success, which is heartwarming for an old deejay. But more important, you'll understand the spiritual journey that Minowa has undertaken as well, which has been inspirational for me. I hope it can be for you, too, even if you're not a fan of his music. A few years ago Minowa and I discussed his meditation practice and how it had helped him deal with the stress of touring and raising a family and financing it all through his own label, all the myriad elements of the profession that he had acquired around him. I gulped, thinking that if it can help him, it might do wonders for me, as I have none of those massive concerns. Stilling the mind a little bit every day over the past few years has helped me enormously.

Being on a similar path has made me connect with Cloud

Cult in a special way, and perhaps it's impossible for me to be unbiased. When the album *Love* came out early in 2013, I immediately declared that it would be on my top ten at the end of the year, and it was. But even more I thought it was the band's best work ever—and how many times do you say that about a band that has been around as long as they have, especially one that has done it themselves, without help from an industry that collapsed around them? Except perhaps for a little help from good old radio stations like ours, who champion authenticity. Who still believe there is an alternative way to do things long after those cynical days of the "alternative nation" have waned. Yes, who still believe in love.

I came to Minnesota in 1992, aware of the state's reputation for producing such talent as Dylan, Prince, The Replacements, and Hüsker Dü. These artists set a high standard of success that inspired a new generation of young musicians to believe that they could survive and thrive by following their own muse, in their own ways. Making a living as a musician has become harder since I arrived here, and yet a wide variety of artists in all genres have figured out new ways to measure success and to create their own new business models. None have done this more drastically or profoundly than Cloud Cult. Indeed, even as a fan I had no idea how innovative and progressive they were when they started until I read this book. Seeing their success from the confines of the local music scene was exhilarating enough. Put into a larger context, it's truly mind-blowing.

Introduction

Conversations hush. Rhythmic clapping and callouts for the band come from the balcony and the tightly packed floor—fans are sensing that it's nearly time. When the screen in front of the stage begins to rise, band members walk out and take up their instruments, greeted by a near-deafening roar of excitement and devotion, which only gets louder when the lights go down and the opening horn and string-heavy melody of "Unexplainable Stories" begins. The music builds, and when the guitars and drums join the strings and horns, when the spotlights come on, when the painters begin spinning their easels and throwing paint on their canvases—the crowd goes wild again.

After touring the East and West Coasts in support of its new album *Light Chasers* (2010), Cloud Cult has returned home for two CD release shows at Minneapolis's famed First Avenue, the main 1980s venue for Prince and the setting of *Purple Rain*, home to forty years of great shows by the likes of the Allman Brothers and The Replacements. Cloud Cult's time on the road has made it a tight band, but one of my favorite moments occurs when Craig Minowa tells a story. "Back in 2003," he says to the audience, "Scott West and I were here passing out CDs of our band to the staff and asking if we could get a gig, and we were kicked out for harassing them. And now here we are playing two sold-out shows"—the crowd cheers—"and we even got a star on First Ave's wall!" The concert is celebratory from the beginning, not just because it's a CD release party but because new life (the birth of Nova Minowa, Connie and Craig's son) fueled the album's creation. The next morning I read a posting on the band's website from a concertgoer: "I've been to thirty Cloud Cult shows over the years," she writes, "and I've cried at every one of them, but last night, for the first time, my tears were tears of joy."

Cloud Cult fans often have deeply personal connections to the band, in part because the band's origin story begins in tragic loss. Aspiring musician and dedicated environmentalist Craig Minowa had made three records but had no audience beyond friends and family when in 2002 his beloved young son, Kaidin, died unexpectedly without apparent cause. Minowa sank deeply into a paralyzing grief, able to write only songs expressing his pain and loss, songs that he later shaped into the album *They Live on the Sun* (2003). Other records followed, philosophical and spiritual journeyings released on his own label, Earthology Records. And so began the slow rise of Cloud Cult, the *Pitchfork*- and NPR-acclaimed indie rock band widely regarded as one of the most principled and idealistic groups in music.

In his recent best-selling book *The Shallows,* Nicholas Carr argues that the Internet changes how we think, learn, and feel, distracting us from thinking hard or absorbing knowledge and teaching us to browse, to skim, to flit. Something similar, many people believe, is happening with the switch in music from vinyl albums and record players to MP3 downloads and computers, with their enormous capacities to store music and their ability to play songs as a random shuffle. Music lovers might own more music than ever before and be familiar with more band names and more genres of music, but they know this music "shallowly," to use Carr's term. They flit from song to song on YouTube, perhaps, not always knowing about the band or even hearing the music complexly as much as getting into the visual effects. Such listen-

ers may enjoy music very much, but they don't have a meaningful relationship with individual songs, and they rarely know entire
albums.

Cloud Cult fans may have encountered the band through
the Internet or had their interest piqued by a particular song,
but they tend to develop a deep, not shallow, relationship to the
band's music. Perhaps the fans' devotion to the music comes
because so many learn about Craig Minowa's personal story,
which means that each album is understood as part of a life pro-
gression, and therefore fans tend to know albums. Or perhaps
the connection arises simply because Minowa writes songs that
invite reflection and emotion. I began this project on Cloud Cult
in part because I wanted to understand the strong devotion that
fans have to this band. In my e-mail messages and conversations,
I've been struck by one consistent chord: passionate fans admire
with all their hearts how Cloud Cult has made a nearly seamless whole of living lives, being artists, and running a business. "I
wrote to the website, and Craig personally answered me back!"
they say over and over. "While many corporations and bands give
lip service to promoting environmentalism or any social cause,
Cloud Cult has never strayed from their principles," fans say. "The
Minowas' personal tragedy has made them more open to mine,"
I hear.

Many fans who care so deeply seem not only to have witnessed Minowa's musical journey with its raising of profound
questions about spiritual matters, but likewise to have experienced the Cloud Cult journey as part of their own. In between a
few of the chapters, I have placed thirty-five unedited fan testimonials about the band that demonstrate these intertwined jour-
neys of musicians and listeners.

We have been hearing for more than ten years now about
the death of the music industry, about how labels are losing

money. The last part is true, but the first is not. The model for labels, as well as singers and bands, has changed drastically with the Internet and capabilities of file sharing and MP3 downloads. Very few young people today buy albums. An NPR intern and college radio deejay, Emily White, who is an avid music listener and concertgoer, unintentionally caused a huge stir recently when she wrote that of her music library of eleven thousand songs, she had probably paid for only fifteen albums. (To her credit, she didn't illegally download most of them, and she does support bands by going to numerous concerts and buying T-shirts.) The replies to her piece, and there were thousands, ranged from the righteous to the astute, the latter exemplified by David Lowery's long reply to White that argued that many young people will buy hardware and software, car insurance, and lattes but don't want to pay even for the music they love—and so artists just don't make much money, at least not in the traditional way with album sales. The album-buying audience for any particular band is usually small, particularly by standards of mainstream pop and rock of past decades—we will never again see the likes of Def Leppard selling 450,000 albums in one day (or more than 1 million in a week), as they did with *Hysteria*. The weekly top album now might sell only 50,000 copies, and the falloff from there is steep.

Everything in recent years that has cut into the profits of the music industry—digital recordings, Internet downloads, the iPod, social media—has enabled the growth of new music. It's much easier now to make a record, and there are lots of venues to play, especially smaller ones, because new ways of sharing music and communicating directly to fans help deliver an audience. Rich music scenes have exploded in numerous cities (Brooklyn, Austin, Minneapolis, Chapel Hill, Seattle, among the many), where bands on small labels know one another and interact with their fans directly.

Music lovers today live in a golden age. Whatever your taste, you can find great music. Pop, hip-hop, rock, country, and folk music have each split into numerous niches and borrow heavily from one another, resulting in more experimentation. Pigeonholing a scene or a band can hardly be done now, for radio stations or major labels. Within my favorite genre of music, indie rock, there are great bands with a wide range of styles and sounds—bands such as Arcade Fire, The National, Neutral Milk Hotel, Bon Iver, Grizzly Bear, Iron and Wine, the Black Keys, Alabama Shakes, the Decemberists, Rilo Kiley, Andrew Bird. That indie rock listeners could make their own lists of favorite bands and include none of those on mine attests to this golden age. This book is not about the indie rock scene, but Cloud Cult's story of making its own way outside the commercial market is similar to the stories of all these bands, who have heavily valued artistic freedom and have made great music and found an audience.

All passionate fans of particular bands remember the moment when they became captivated and began a relationship with the band's music. My moment with Cloud Cult came on a beautiful afternoon, sitting in my office in front of my computer, looking out the window at vibrant fall colors. I teach literature and environmental studies at St. Olaf College in Northfield, Minnesota, and occasionally I teach music in the context of performance poetry or protest literature. For years students had been telling me about an acclaimed indie band they were sure I would like, and after one such conversation I finally went to the Cloud Cult website and rather randomly clicked on a video of the song "When Water Comes to Life."

The song opens with a violin playing a simple melody, which is repeated, then a cello and flute come in over the top of the violin. When an oboe enters, introducing a short melody line that becomes the melodic leitmotif, the cello and violin change to pizzicato, carrying the rhythm instead of the melody. A trombone, French horn, and bassoon enrich the oboe's melody line, and for the first minute and twenty-six seconds of the song, you might imagine you're hearing a new piece for orchestra, one announcing its pensive mood in beautiful melodies and harmonies. And then Minowa begins singing in a shaky, vulnerable voice:

> And when the angels come, they'll cut you down the
>   middle,
> To see if you're still there, to see if you're still there.
> And underneath your ribs, they'll find a heart-shaped
>   locket,
> An old photograph, of you in Daddy's arms.
> And then they'll sew you closed, and give you back to
>   the water,
> From where we're all born, from where we're all born.

Minowa goes on to say that the "you" will paradoxically be both leper and healer, both hero and tragedy. The second half of this song then turns literal, not figurative. The body will be sewn closed, Minowa sings, and burned, and all that will be left is sand crystals, two tiny handfuls, "all the rest is water, water." As the song progresses, the music becomes more and more intense, as does the singing when bandmates join Minowa. Melodic singing becomes a fierce chanting. The cello plays a fast, low rhythm; guitar, synthesizer, and drums come crashing in; voices merge. Everything combines to give the song a strong melodic energy and drive that tells us we will all eventually return to water, ready to begin again the cycle of life and death. "All you need to know," Minowa sings repeatedly, is that "you were born of water, you are made of water." At the song's end, I suddenly realized that I had just listened to a brilliant piece about a child's autopsy and cremation.

The more listens I gave "When Water Comes to Life," the better the song got: richer in musical textures, more complex in theme. How, I thought, could someone make a moving, beautiful song out of such tragic circumstance? How does this song bring out tragedy's deep sorrow yet ultimately feel hopeful? "When Water Comes to Life" led me to other songs, and I bought one of the band's albums, and then bought all of them. Not just the music grabbed my attention. Learning more about the band, I came to admire Cloud Cult for the principles it practices, for the attempts to fashion a business model that creates a zero carbon footprint for both recording and touring. The website planetgreen.com, in an article on the five most eco-conscious musicians, lists the likes of stars such as Jack Johnson and Pearl Jam, but says that Cloud Cult, while not famous like the others, is "definitely the greenest." Sarah Young, longtime cellist for the band, puts it this way: "You can't really say that Cloud Cult is music without saying that it's an environmental movement, too."

An environmental movement, a rock band that models the do-it-yourself indie ethos, a unique concert band that employs two live painters on stage, exemplary people who in part overcame their grief over their young son's death by making incredible music: Craig Minowa and his band Cloud Cult are all these things and more. Here's their story.

Seeds

lying sixty-five miles due south of Minneapolis, Owatonna is representative of an iconic upper Midwest small town, the kind that Garrison Keillor has made famous and made fun of on *A Prairie Home Companion*. The Straight River winds through Owatonna, and Bridge Street joins the west and east sides. Main Street runs through the middle of town and has turn-of-the-century buildings. Well-maintained neighborhoods surround downtown, with class divisions distinguished only subtly by the size of houses and lots. Known mostly as an agricultural center because of the fertile farmland surrounding it, Owatonna also serves as headquarters for several large companies, including Federated Insurance and Viracon, an international company that makes high-performance architectural glass products. With outstanding parks and good schools, Owatonna was a nice place to raise children in the 1970s, when Victor Richardson and his wife, Clarice, moved to town.

Vic and Clarice had gotten married and then lived for three years in Jeffers, Minnesota, where Vic was an agricultural arts teacher and Clarice a nurse. They moved to Owatonna with their oldest child, Melanie, and their four-month-old son, Craig, who was soon followed by a baby sister, Janelle. Vic and Clarice began the slow process of settling deeply into a community, a process that included buying a modest house on a pleasant street. For some people, tracing their journey from the past to the present is a meandering path, a series of personal choices and random events that only incrementally and with hindsight reveals a direction, an arrival. But in many ways, the band Cloud Cult comes rather directly from Craig Richardson's early interests that are connected to this boyhood house (it would not be until his marriage in 1998 that he would take the last name of Minowa). In many ways, Craig had a typical boyhood, building model airplanes and playing with his sisters and children in the neighborhood, but even in his early years he had a marked interest in the nonhuman world, as many of his mother's memories about him show.

"Craig was early on interested in the stars," his mother recalls, "and so one year we got him a telescope, which he loved." Or this: "He always cared for anything living, trees or animals. He hated even to kill bugs. He had an environmental conscience early in his life, as a teenager. He didn't get it from us. We learned from him."

She describes how from the time he became verbal, Craig could mimic sounds that he heard in nature. "It was just so cute," she says, smiling in remembrance.

The house that Minowa grew up in sits in an attractive neighborhood of carefully mown lawns and shade trees, recently painted houses, and cars in garages. Minowa attributes the beginnings of his love for nature to two box elder trees that towered in his backyard. He chose to indirectly memorialize the trees with his first solo album, *The Shade Project,* in part because he was picked on as a child when he had a head injury and for a time had to wear a helmet: "I was one of the only kids that could climb those trees. So I spent a lot of time up there just thinking. It was one of the few places I felt safe. I would go back to those trees even in my college years, looking for insights. Anyway, *The Shade Project* is called that because of the protection of the shade of those trees. Ultimately, the music became my 'shade,' so hunkering down in the studio was a comparable feeling to being in those trees."

The house is five blocks from Kaplan's Woods: 225 acres of trees and paths and a lake, secluded and even a bit wild, nothing like a suburban park. Minowa hung out a lot in the woods, and there he had a life-shaping epiphany. "I remember skipping church on an Easter morning back when I was a teenager, which was a huge no-no in our family," Minowa recalls. "It was a really beautiful spring day, and I wanted to go to the woods instead. I spent the whole morning in Kaplan's Woods and had a profound spiritual experience. It was a big turning point for me, because it was a realization of how I had spent so many years of my childhood contained inside the four walls of the church, which is where I was supposed to find God. But from then on, I found I felt closest to God when I was alone in nature." If the phrase "geography is destiny" is true about cities, whether that relates to lying along transportation routes or having a good harbor or idyllic weather, the phrase is also true about individuals, and the Richardsons' move to Owatonna and purchase of a house near Kaplan's Woods profoundly shaped Minowa.

As with nature, music was an abiding presence in Minowa's early life. Clarice played piano at home and in their church, and the Richardsons encouraged their children by providing them with private lessons. Owatonna has always had a strong arts and music program, where all children in elementary school are encouraged to join the orchestra and band, and Minowa went through the school system playing the upright bass in the orchestra. As a high-school student, he dreamed of combining his two passions by composing music for National Geographic shows or writing soundtracks for environmentally themed movies. Encouraged by a highly respected orchestral bass player, Minowa decided to go to the University of North Texas and major in music composition.

But then occurred one of those moments that changes the course of a life.

When he told his high school orchestra conductor, Bruce Wood, about his plans, Wood explained that the classical music composition field is highly competitive and difficult to earn a living in; he recommended going into a profession such as instrument repair or teaching. Minowa looked up to Wood, who was an excellent teacher and who had inspired him to go into music in the first place, and hearing that made Minowa change his plans. He was playing in an alternative rock band at the time, and two of those band members were going to college at nearby Mankato State University. Minowa decided to go to school there and give the band a chance at the same time.

The band, Counterpoint, had come together serendipitously. Jeff DuVernay, the drummer, recalls hearing Minowa before meeting him: "The first time I heard Craig play any music was in 1990, several months before Counterpoint formed and before the two of us had officially met each other. There was a local music store in Owatonna called Tones Music that sold and rented musical instruments, including guitars, drums, and orchestral instruments. I would often go there to play some of their acoustic guitars. One time, Craig was in there doing the same thing but on an acoustic bass. I noticed that he was playing the bass line to The Cure song 'Just Like Heaven.' I later discovered that Craig was a huge Cure fan—this was the only band that we covered at our shows."

Perhaps the serendipity began even earlier, when Josh Lukkes, from Brookings, South Dakota, moved with his mother to Owatonna and got a job at Pizza Hut. There, at the work station where employees made pizzas and put them in the ovens, Lukkes met, in his words, a "gangly, acned orchestra-dork"—Craig Richardson. They began talking music together and decided to start a band, which became Sons of Silence. They never played gigs but did record some original songs.

DuVernay had been playing music and working at a local video store with Scott West, and through a mutual friend, West met Lukkes at a dorm party at Mankato State that fall. "Simply put," DuVernay says, "after talking music that night, Josh and Scott decided that the four of us should get together and play some music. The first time we played was over winter break of 1990 down in my parents' basement in Owatonna. A keyboardist, Teresa Arendsee, a high school friend of Josh's from South Dakota, joined us for our initial jam. After a few weeks, Craig decided to form a band with us, and we practiced in my parents' basement every Sunday, starting January 1991."

Counterpoint's first official show was May 8 at Shades, a small venue in the Mankato State student union. Minowa got very nervous before the show—then and at other shows that followed, he would need to leave the band and be alone before they went on stage. But the band showed promise, and the guys were excited, and they spent the summer writing original songs. Minowa typically wrote the lyrics, often with the help of Lukkes, and together the two of them would craft something from a rough idea and bring it to the rest of the band. DuVernay remembers that even from behind the drums, he would make suggestions for guitar parts, and they would give him ideas for different drumbeats and rhythms. Occasionally, part of a song would come spontaneously from jamming during a band practice.

In September 1991, Counterpoint self-recorded its album *Within.* A small indie magazine based in Minneapolis, *Cake,* reviewed the album positively, saying that the band sounded like The Cure. That fall, Counterpoint played a second show at Shades, and in spring played at other nearby colleges and even made it to the 7th Street Entry, a small venue attached to the legendary First Avenue in Minneapolis. Counterpoint was off and running, but Minowa's one year in Mankato at the state university was not. Classes weren't challenging enough for him. And then he quit the band, in part because of his horrible stage fright, in part because he didn't like the egoism of the performance scene. An introvert, often a loner, he preferred simply to write music at home.

Counterpoint ended, but except for DuVernay, finishing his last year of high school in Owatonna, the band members were all leaving Mankato for Minneapolis: that summer, Minowa arranged to transfer to the University of Minnesota; West enrolled at the Minnesota College of Art and Design to study painting; Lukkes enrolled at the University of Minnesota, though he soon dropped out to pursue his dream of making it in the music business. Minowa immersed himself in his college classes, but the most important events of that fall happened outside the classroom. Home in Owatonna one weekend for a family gathering, he met his younger sister's best friend, Connie Staska, whom Janelle had invited along for the ride to take Minowa back to school. Connie was only fifteen at the time but already someone with a strong, unique perspective on the world. Very artistic, pretty, passionate about music and nature, she immediately caught Minowa's attention. But because Connie was so young, his mother says, he held back from asking her out.

Minowa missed playing music with his friends, and so he agreed to reform the band—the other significant event of that fall. The band chose a new name, Eden's Ashes, and in early 1993 went into a studio and recorded a three-song EP, *Hallowed Greed,* which created some local press buzz. Over the next few months, Eden's Ashes played regularly: in Minneapolis at McCready's Pub and for parties in the warehouse district; another show at 7th

Street Entry; at the University of Wisconsin, Madison. Though the band appeared to be making it, West's ambitions in music were always tempered by his interest in painting, and Minowa not only didn't like the dive bars but was frustrated by his inability to meld his two passions, music and environmentalism. For Eden's Ashes, Minowa often wrote songs with preachy environmental lyrics, and he'd make information sheets about environmental issues and pass them out at shows, which didn't go over well with the audience and caused some tension in the band. But Lukkes had big ambitions. "As a young man," he remembers, "college was my backup plan for becoming a rock star. Eden's Ashes was never a sideline; it was the main thing." He believed that the band had enough talent to go to the top of the indie rock world.

So how does a rock band begin and make a career with music? The archetypal story goes something like this: young kids get together, write songs, practice in someone's garage, score a few gigs in local clubs. A talent agent sees them, recognizes genius, signs them to an exploitive contract that nevertheless allows the band to get into the recording studio, where it makes an album that the record label promotes heavily. After a single gets played on commercial radio, the album hits the *Billboard* charts and is reviewed by rock journalists. A career begins, a career of wealth, fame, and rock and roll.

The moment that aspiring indie rock musicians wait for occurred when Eden's Ashes got a letter expressing interest from an A&R rep at TVT Records, a prominent alt-rock label riding high at the time with the band Nine Inch Nails. But being on the verge of success means you have to decide what that success actually entails, as well as what you'll do to make it happen. Just when Eden's Ashes looked like they might take the next step, Minowa packed up his belongings and left for Alaska to work on a fishing boat. The band couldn't continue without its lead singer and one of its principal songwriters, and when TVT Records was told that the band had temporarily disbanded, the label dropped all interest.

Humans make complex choices by weighing conscious and unconscious factors; major decisions in life are rarely clear-cut, and Minowa's leaving the band certainly fits that description. He was only twenty years old, trying to avoid stepping onto a career path about which he was ambivalent. When he got to Seattle and learned that there were no jobs on fishing boats in Alaska, he ended up going home to Owatonna. His choice looked like failure, but then occurred one of those chance events wherein one door that gets closed by a decision—returning from Seattle rather than going on to Alaska—opens another door. Connie Staska at that point had turned sixteen, and a friend had told her that someone was interested in her. "I later found out it was Craig," Connie recalls, "and so I decided to pay him a visit and ask if he wanted to go on a bike ride later that night, well, at three in the morning. We did, it was magical, and from that point on we started dating."

Because Connie was in high school and Craig was at the university, they had a long-distance relationship for two years, talking on the phone nearly every night and seeing each other most weekends. Occasionally, they would manage to make a brief connection during the week, as the following story from Connie demonstrates: "My Arts Magnet class was attending a play at the Guthrie Theater in Minneapolis on a Wednesday afternoon. The play was finished, and we were heading onto the bus to go back to Owatonna. The bus started to roll away from the curb when out of nowhere, here comes Craig riding his bike (which he fondly called 'Horse') right up next to the bus and to my window, where panting and frantically peddling to keep up with the moving bus, he threw a love letter into my window. He then proceeded to just ride off. He told me that night that he rode all the way across town, several miles, as fast as he could. A few seconds later, he would have missed me, and he could have also killed himself riding along that big bus like that." Like the scene from *Say Anything* where John Cusack plays "In Your Eyes" on a boom box under Ione Skye's bedroom window, Minowa's delivery of a love letter seems like a quintessential gesture from a romantic youth.

When Minowa returned in fall of 1993 to the University of Minnesota, he continued to wrestle with choosing a major: the dream of pursuing music composition was still alive, but he was also considering environmental science. "After about a year of going back and forth between majors," Minowa recollects, "I had this deep meditative day in the woods down by the Minnesota River, and I called on the universe to give me guidance. I came out of the woods with the decision to pursue the environmental sciences." Wanting to leave the world better off than if he hadn't been born, he believed that pursuing an environmentalism career would be the best choice for making positive change.

Minowa spent six years in college before graduating, going only part-time as he supported himself by working numerous low-paying jobs. He also interned with environmental nonprofit groups, doing everything from phone canvassing to aquatic exotic species investigation to helping organize Earth Day festivals. He enjoyed most the opportunity to bring emotion to an environmental message. For a similar reason, his favorite classes focused on the philosophical and moral aspects of environmentalism. But over these years, the struggle remained that has never left him over how to combine environmental passions with music—choosing a major did not end the internal conflict, nor did it place him on the usual student path of classes and socializing and having fun on weekends.

Minowa's way of dealing with his anxiety surrounding the breakup of Eden's Ashes was a return to writing and recording on his own, without performing. The solo work that would become *The Shade Project* began in earnest during his third year in college and would consume him for nearly three years. When he wasn't in class or at a job, Minowa was in his apartment, where he set up his recording equipment in a closet. He'd write music, play instruments, hit the record button over and over. He'd write song lyrics while listening to lectures. Some days, walking to catch the bus, he'd get a great idea for something in a song he was working on, and he'd sprint back to his apartment to record it and miss class altogether. Discussing the writing of *The Shade Project,* Minowa says that at some point it became apparent to him that he had a serious problem: "I'd begin recording in the morning and then it'd be the next morning, and I wouldn't have eaten anything, and I'd be just shaking. . . . It was bad, but it was good, too. With *The Shade Project* I felt I totally lost myself, for the first time in my life." For someone who had decided after deep introspection that he was going to pursue environmental studies and not music, he was acting deeply conflicted.

In the epic poem *Childe Harold's Pilgrimage,* Lord Byron penned lines that capture beautifully the feelings of alienated, sensitive romantic youth:

> There is a pleasure in the pathless woods.
> There is a rapture on the lonely shore.
> There is society, where none intrudes
> By the deep sea, and music in its roar:
> I love not man the less, but Nature more.

The "I" of Minowa's songs in *The Shade Project* shares such a view, turning to the nonhuman world of animals and earth for identification and understanding: the speaker is "formed of earth" in "Only Dirt," and in "Call Me Back," he says, "I feel myself in the sky above." "He makes the leaves his feathers," he sings in one song, and in another: "Feel the flowers on the inside / But outside's black, so don't go back." He longs to escape human society, saying in "Secret Place": "Deep in my shade / I am so safe / I am not afraid." In only one song, "Sleeping Days," does the speaker connect with other humans. But there he falls in love first with an ivory princess and then a green-leaf nymph, hardly flesh-and-blood women, and love is short. Only in death do the lovers stay together: "I'll meet you deep, in sweetest sleep / And you and me, we will be one."

The songs aren't directly about environmental issues, nor, because of the music's sound, does *The Shade Project* seem anything like a nature album, the kind sold as relaxation therapy in New Age stores, where one might hear whale noises and blowing winds set against flutes and violins. The songs are neither pretty nor straightforward rock music. They have prerecorded drums and a bass line, but the rhythm section often exists less to create a backbeat and more to establish a ritualistic beat, as in African drumming. Songs are filled with ambient noises, tempo shifts, and near-discordant juxtapositions of guitar and computerized instruments. Some songwriters or bands burst out of the gate young with a major album, but *The Shade Project* is apprentice work that matters because of what it taught the would-be craftsman.

During the years that Minowa wrote and recorded the songs that became *The Shade Project,* he believed that he would just write albums and never perform live. At this time, in 1996, the music revolution that would take place when digital files could be shared over the Internet was in the near future, and so the next step was to get signed, though not to one of the major labels, which still controlled much of the industry but would be totally uninterested in something so noncommercial, but to a small label.

The seeds of the indie rock explosion and the prominence

of small labels were planted in the mid-1970s with the emergence of punk rock in the United Kingdom—a loud, crude, and raw music. Emphasizing direct and immediate connection between the band and the listener, emphasizing strong emotions such as anger, frustration, and rage, punk music had no place on major labels or commercial radio. And so a new ethos in music, DIY, was born, an ethos that argued rebellion against those who controlled the music industry, against consulting firms who decided what should be played on commercial radio, against all the conventional social rules of how to move forward with a business.

The great Southern California punk rock band Black Flag released its records on the SST label, founded in 1978 by Greg Ginn, lead guitarist of Black Flag, to put out the band's records. SST would go on to release influential records by Minutemen, Dinosaur Jr., Sonic Youth, Hüsker Dü, and Meat Puppets. In Washington, D.C., Ian MacKaye and Jeff Nelson founded Dischord Records in 1980 as a way to press and distribute the album *Minor Disturbance* from their first band, the Teen Idles, who became Minor Threat. Dischord Records would release landmark albums by numerous bands, including Government Issue and Fugazi. In the middle of the country, Tesco Vee, who began the fanzine *Touch and Go,* replaced his zine with a label when his band, the Meatmen, needed to produce a record. Touch and Go Records would eventually move to Chicago and become an important indie label, releasing albums by Butthole Surfers and the Jesus Lizard. Laura Ballance and Mac McCaughan began Merge Records in Chapel Hill, North Carolina, in 1989 in part to put out records by their band, Superchunk; Merge later released great albums by then-unknown bands such as Neutral Milk Hotel, the Magnetic Fields, Spoon, and Lambchop. Win Butler, looking for a label for his first record, thought of Merge as his ideal because of whom they produced—Arcade Fire, even after its huge critical and commercial successes, has stayed with Merge. What all these labels shared was scorn for the usual modes of production, publicity, and reliance on commercial radio. Indie labels wanted their artists to be beholden to no one.

People can argue for hours about the semantics of the terms *indie* or *alternative*—and music critics and bloggers have done so—but in essence the movement was a counterreaction to the dominance in the music industry of a handful of major labels and the corporate thinking that ran those labels, primarily the effort to make as much money for the shareholders as could be made. What the consolidation of the industry and the narrowing of the music's sound accomplished was the rise of alternatives: alternative labels and alternative music. If a band's music appealed only to a small audience and would never get played on commercial radio, the band had to find a small label to help them out. The role of small labels gained national attention in the late 1980s when Bruce Pavitt and Jonathan Poneman, who founded the indie rock label Sub Pop and began ingeniously marketing its unknown bands as "the Seattle Sound," flew the influential British music journalist Everett True to Seattle to write an article on the local music. True, and later the British press in general, became enamored with what they called the Seattle grunge scene. American music journalists followed the British, and major label executives began heading to the Northwest. Soundgarden, a Sub Pop group, signed with A&M Records, Alice in Chains with Columbia. But it was Geffen Records' release of a former Sub Pop band's new album *Nevermind* that made Nirvana a household name by flying up the *Billboard* charts to number one. Rather than looking for unknown talent whom they could steer from the beginning, major labels began looking to bands who had already released an album or two on an indie label, bands who might already have a regional reputation, and who certainly had more experience in making records and touring.

It might seem that major labels discovering they could

make money off bands who once had only an underground, non-pop audience would have hurt the small indie labels. But artists quickly found out that signing with major labels often meant that while they could spend much more money—on making the album, on staying in expensive hotels and driving in custom buses while on tour—they didn't really end up with more money. They were often literally in debt to their labels, who could then exert artistic control or even just drop the band when a new album didn't sell immediately. And there were always numerous bands who fit no particular musical genre and whose music seemed alien to what was played on commercial radio, making them unmarketable for a major label. Such bands had to seek out an indie label if they wanted to get help with production and distribution.

This story of indie labels supporting outside-the-mainstream music was what Craig Minowa knew. Looking for such labels, he checked out a book at the library that had mailing addresses, even though the book was years outdated so he knew that many of the addresses would have changed or disappeared. A friend who worked at a small record label told Minowa that he received a high quantity of unsolicited submissions, and unless the cassette caught his eye, it often went into the garbage unlistened to. Minowa wanted to be as environmentally friendly as possible, and at the time there wasn't access to recycled products, so he used dried leaves for padding in the packages and reused envelopes with stickers placed over the old addresses. He figured this might catch someone's eye enough to listen to the album.

Minowa mailed *The Shade Project* out to one hundred small record labels, and a few weeks later he started receiving rejection letters. One woman actually wrote back to say that she was repulsed to open a package and see dry leaves inside, that it was like shipping a box of dirt, and that he needed to be more professional. A few small labels wrote and said they enjoyed the music; two said they might be taking more bands on in the coming year and asked Minowa to check back. The small but noted Bright Green Records in Chicago actually committed to signing him, but said that he needed to have a live band because there was no way to make it in the music business without touring. This news was not what Minowa wanted to hear, given his previous stage fright performing with Counterpoint and Eden's Ashes, but he also wanted to have *The Shade Project* out there in the world. So he began to recruit band members.

Minowa had performed all the instruments on *The Shade Project,* so creating a live band was a matter of finding musicians who could replicate the sound of the album on stage. Sarah Young, longtime cellist for Cloud Cult, tells the story of how she began playing music with Minowa: "I was in the campus orchestra at the University of Minnesota, the orchestra for the non-music majors . . . and I saw a sign that I believe was in crayon, that said 'signed band seeking cellist.' Craig interviewed me and had me play the cello, and then he said 'all right.'" She was in, followed soon by other musicians.

Minowa now had his live band, but when he contacted Bright Green Records to let them know he was ready to sign and start touring, they apologized and said they had gone bankrupt and closed their doors. At that point, Minowa continued conversations with other labels while doing some show bookings himself. The band, called Fable, never actually ended up signing with anyone. Though it did get some gigs, Minowa's stress about performing live had grown to the extent that he was having panic attacks before shows. He simply couldn't be the center of attention. He broke up the band.

Although Minowa's musical career once again was going nowhere, his relationship with Connie Staska was flourishing. After
her graduation from Owatonna High School in June 1995, Connie began higher education at the Minneapolis College of Art and
Design (MCAD) that fall. She remembers thinking as early as third
grade that she wanted to be an artist. Her mother says that Connie, as a girl, always had music playing and drew or painted on
every piece of paper in the house and even on the walls and ceil-
ing. Though Connie developed interests during her teen years in
philosophy and spirituality, "at some point," she recalls now with
a laugh, "I figured I could probably make a better living as an artist than a philosopher." When she began at MCAD, she and Craig
moved in together.

The next two years for Craig were full of study and part-
time jobs connected in some way to environmental issues. In
May 1998 he graduated from the University of Minnesota with
a bachelor of science degree in environmental sciences, with a
focus on water resources and sustainable agriculture. Looking
for full-time work, Minowa landed a job as a "tree surgeon." He
quickly learned that the job consisted of driving around in a pesticide truck and spraying trees whether they needed it or not. The
company was breaking multiple laws pertaining to safe pesticide
use; drift would float into neighboring yards, onto kids' toys and
family pets; the company told Minowa to fake-diagnose trees to
land extra spraying jobs. He didn't last a week, and when he left
he wrote a long letter to the company with recommendations on
how they could benefit from using integrated pesticide manage-
ment practices and how they were breaking the laws and what
they could do to reduce their environmental impact. They ignored
him. Shortly after, Minowa got a job doing various water measure-
ments on the river in Eau Claire, Wisconsin. The power company
there, working on relicensing, had commissioned the work. It took

little talent or preparation to do the readings, so Minowa felt that
his education was a waste for a job like that. His disillusionment
was even greater because most of the work crew seemed uninterested in doing anything but collecting a paycheck. "There was
never a meaningful deep conversation," Minowa recalls. "I think I
had some pretty high and unrealistic ideals about what it meant
to work in the environmental field."

Minowa believed his next job, as a sales position for a company selling whole-house water purification systems, "would be
good, honest work helping people protect their families from tox-
ins in the water supply." Immersed in training on techniques to
get people to purchase expensive equipment, he was disgusted
by the sales tricks. He told his concerns to his sales trainer, and
the man responded by pointing at his expensive car and saying
how nice it was to pay bills. At his first sales call, Minowa actually
started to cry when giving the pitch and apologized to the family
members for wasting their time. The next day he went in to speak
to the owner of the company and told him that his purification
systems were a good product but that the sales aspect was mis-
leading. Minowa was shocked when the owner said, "People like
you make me sick." Other jobs followed, less in the business world
than in environmental education, but the gap between Minowa's
ideals and the practices he encountered was still large. He finally
realized that he was desperately unhappy, and so one night he
stayed up until morning writing a step-by-step list of "What I
need to do to start making a living doing music." The jobs got no
better, for the most part, but at least they weren't disillusioning.
Minowa worked as a wedding deejay, as a maintenance man at his
apartment complex, and as an entertainer at children's birthday
parties, dressing up in costumes, dancing, doing face painting
and balloon animals.

Most important during this time, Craig and Connie got

married on August 7, 1998, in an outdoor ceremony in a nature reserve. The wedding and reception were completely personalized. They had a big tent for guests. Connie made hanging candles, and they draped trees in white lights. Connie and Craig were both interested in Native American culture, and an Indian shaman married them. They adopted a new last name, keeping their surnames as middle names and adding Minowa, which means "moving voice." Craig's mother, Clarice, remembers the day as being a beautiful wedding, melding art and music and ritual. "The weather had been iffy all day," she recalls, "but during the ceremony, the sun came out and lit everything up, almost like a blessing on this marriage."

Four months later, Connie graduated from MCAD with a bachelor of fine arts degree in painting and drawing. As soon as she was done with school, the Minowas moved to Duluth, in large part because they liked the progressiveness of the community, as well as the nearby nature of Lake Superior and the north woods. Connie began working as a field organizer and fair-trade coordinator for the nonprofit group Organic Consumers Association, and the Minowas entertained the idea of opening an eco-home store. Craig continued to deejay weddings in Duluth. When he got a part-time job as marketing manager at the Whole Foods Co-op, he finally felt like he was working with like-minded people.

Minowa's part-time jobs were only marginally satisfying to a smart, well-educated, talented twenty-something, but they did allow him to devote more time to a new artistic project that he had begun, a project that would eventually become the album *Who Killed Puck?* The album's title references Shakespeare's famous comedy *A Midsummer Night's Dream*, a play that takes place largely in the forest where young lovers from Athens flee a tyrannical father, where working-class Athenians who are amateur actors practice, and where supernatural characters reside, including Puck, who makes mischief with the lovers and actors. The forest is the Faeries' world, one where dreams and confusions and love intertwine, separate from real-life consequences. In the liner notes to *Who Killed Puck?*, Minowa says that his record is the story of a "modern day Puck" plucked from a Shakespearean dream and "reborn into the industrialized world"—into the United States in the late twentieth century, a world of overpopulation, high-technology, and environmental disasters. In this album the killing of Puck implies a killing of human characteristics such as art, spontaneity, and play.

Who Killed Puck? didn't begin as a musical project but rather a film treatment. In the liner notes, Minowa writes that the album may be the first movie soundtrack that has no movie. He says that when he was younger he dreamed of doing soundtracks. When he got an idea for a film but had no money or tools to make it, he could still create a record; he could compose music and sound effects for each scene. "The reason it's a soundtrack to a film that doesn't exist," he says, "is not because of some deep artistic irony. It was pure logistics." With this new idea, Minowa returned to what he was most comfortable with, a solo studio project done simply for the love of music's spirituality, for the love of simply making art: "*Who Killed Puck?* was a music project created completely out of my own inherent need to create. There was zero intention of making a live band. And I wholeheartedly didn't think anyone other than a few friends would ever listen to it."

Many albums are simply collections of songs; in contrast, *Who Killed Puck?* takes the thematic album to its limits—Minowa having created a record that is earnestly about Big Ideas: the negative consequences to the human and nonhuman world of industrialization, Christianity, and consumerism. The seriousness begins with the artwork of the album. On the front cover, spoof ads (Prozac laundry brightener: "Wash Your Blues Away") surround the famous photograph by Diane Arbus *Child with Toy Hand Grenade in Central Park*. The world of this cover is a world that's gone mad, and opening the album to get the disc out, you see reasons why. On the left fold, nuclear smokestacks billow below the mind-blowing discussion of time, in which the "6 days of the book of Genesis" are compared to the "4 billion years of geologic time." In this account, human history begins at three minutes before midnight on the final day, and Christ appears one-quarter of a second before midnight. At one-fortieth of a second before midnight the Industrial Revolution begins, and Minowa ends the diatribe with the following: "We are surrounded by people who think that what we have been doing for one-fortieth of a second can last indefinitely. They are considered normal, but they are stark raving mad." In the album's middle fold, Minowa addresses the negative effects of advertising. Next to a photograph of a young teen peeing in a urinal while looking at ads on the wall and a television playing commercials, Minowa writes that the United States spends more on advertising than on education and that the average child sees thirty thousand commercials each year.

The album's arc follows the birth of a child to his death: from "Where It Starts," "Conception," and "9 Months" to "Puck's Sixth Birthday" to "Who Killed Puck?" and "Close," whose lyric talks about regeneration and then ends with silence for the last eighty seconds of the song. Within this arc, in songs heavily reliant on computer-generated sounds and ambient noise, Minowa attacks American culture for its conformity and obsession with material goods. Puck probably has elements of Minowa's own personal story—having some difficulties as a child, being the outsider, not fitting in, and even getting bullied. "Becoming One of You," for example, is a song about being born, feeling different, and then steering that fear of difference and longing for acceptance into self-denying attempts to talk, breathe, dress, act, and think like the others: "I would do anything / If you would let me be One of you," the boy sings. This song is followed by "Ad Brainwash (Part 1)," in which this need to be like others leads to a keep-up-with-the-Joneses consumerism. Minowa follows "Ad Brainwash" with "Six Days to Madness," linking that consumerism to Christianity. Over a driving guitar, synthesizer, and heavy drumming, Minowa has a man relate in solemn voice the discussion of geologic time and human history, followed shortly by the song "Lies," which attacks Christianity for its elevation of humans above all other creatures and the nonhuman world. Against a background of someone reading the famous chapters from Genesis that give Man dominion over all the animals and everything on earth, Minowa repetitively sings, "These lies will bury us all."

The narrative in *Who Killed Puck?* is difficult to follow, and the songs aren't melodic or subtle, but Minowa's alienation from and fears for the world are easy to see. Humans mistreating the nonhuman world is only part of the problem, as the bigger problem is our disconnect from everything, including feeling. But the album would not make people who are anti-nature or pro-consumerism reconsider their values or positions, nor is the album one that many listeners would enjoy just for the sounds of the songs. The album did leave one lasting impression. In a 2010 interview in *Mayday* magazine, Raul Clement asked where the name Cloud Cult came from, and Minowa replied that "it wasn't ever intended to be the band name. It was the name of the *Who Killed Puck?* studio project and summed up the focus of that album. Cloud Cult is a collection of ancient prophesies that predicted European settlement here in North America and predicted the downfall of the current society at the hands of poorly managed overuse of technology. It basically suggests that our technology is growing faster than our spirituality and that we are getting out of balance."

The album's themes became even more urgent during composition because Connie had become pregnant, and the two of them were about to bring a baby into a world that Craig was portraying as an environmental disaster. But both Craig and Connie were excited and happy about becoming new parents, and a new century was ushered in for them with a defining moment: the birth of Kaidin Staska Richardson Minowa in February 2000. The new parents focused on the baby, parenthood shaping their day-to-day lives as well as their philosophies. "Kaidin helped bring me into the present," Connie says, "and made me more focused on the here and now and less on the past and future. Reality changes when you become a parent."

Craig remembers similar powerful feelings: "I talk about how I can lose myself inside the music, and how I can separate from myself at that level, and parenthood is the only other thing in my life that I've experienced that with, because you totally set yourself aside, and your child is the center of the universe in a great way."

The joy in having Kaidin tempered, to some extent, the difficulties that Minowa was having pursuing his dream of music. "By the time I finished *Who Killed Puck?*, Kaidin was about to be born," Minowa recalls. "Finances were really bad for us, and I was working several part-time jobs and donating blood plasma twice a week just to keep afloat. The possibility of having time or money to pursue the music dream just didn't exist. Again, the Internet music opportunities still weren't there yet, because these were the days of dial-up, so the amount of time and funding you needed to get your music out there was way out of reach for me." Friends nevertheless pushed him to do more than just have the album sit unheard, but the difficulties in doing so were large. There were two big questions: What label would take a chance on a record experimental even for alternative rock? How could

Minowa remain true to his strongly held environmental principles if he gave up control of the record to a label? Small labels who modeled an out-of-the-mainstream, artist-oriented business still used a production process that was decidedly not earth friendly, and so the answer was clear: Craig and Connie together decided to found their own label to produce Craig's music and anyone else's who came to them, but to do so in a new way.

"Earthology Records started," Minowa explains, "out of necessity because there wasn't any compact disc replication place out there that did environmentally friendly CDs. . . . the most popular CD you could get was the plastic one, and a lot of the plastic that they used for that was polyvinyl chloride (PVC), and every disc was shrink-wrapped in PVC. And when you manufacture PVC and dispose of it, you're creating carcinogens and dioxins. When I finished *Who Killed Puck?* and there was a really strong environmental message in it, I felt like it would be goofy to make this really crappy product and put it out there."

Minowa developed the first 100 percent postconsumer recycled compact disc packaging in the United States market. For cases, he went to college bookstores and gave them boxes for students to put their used jewel cases into. He then hand washed each case, made his CD inserts from 100 percent postconsumer recycled paper printed with nontoxic soy ink, and wrapped the cases in nontoxic shrink-wrap. Minowa got *Who Killed Puck?* ready to go without even the production, distribution, and publicity that a small label could give. And it was an enormous task that he was tackling. There were no books then on how to begin a record label or get a career started as an indie band like there are today, like Randy Chertkow and Jason Feehan's *The Indie Band Survival Guide* or Ian Anderson's *Here Come the Regulars,* just two examples that are packed full of solid advice and particular strategies. Years before "sustainability" or "green business" became part of the cultural vernacular, the Minowas were going it alone, figuring out what practices would work with their strong principles.

With no connections that a label gives an artist, Minowa sent *Who Killed Puck?* to some local press. Only one publication responded, the reviewer taking two sentences to say that he didn't understand the album, that it was confusing and had too many genres of music happening from song to song. Minowa was stung by this reaction to a deeply personal album he had worked on for four years. With no way to earn money except by doing multiple, low-paying jobs, with a new baby to support, he could only foresee doing music for the love of it. And he did, finishing a new album, *Dream Music (for little wizards),* that he had begun writing when Connie was pregnant. Craig had researched alpha waves and what they do to brain waves, and how alpha waves can go through the skin and into the womb, and so the album was a set of songs for pregnant women and newborn babies. *Dream Music* sold only a handful of copies, mostly to family and friends, but though his music career was at a standstill, Craig was a happy father.

Wanting to work at home, Minowa had begun a job for a local nonprofit involved in issues that he was passionate about: the Environmental Association for Great Lakes Education. For his position there he had to learn about designing and maintaining websites. At that time, in 2000, user-friendly tools to build your own website didn't exist, and so Minowa had to check books out of the library and teach himself about HTML programming. That work led him in 2001 to a job with the Organic Consumers Association, at first on their website and later as a content creator, building action alerts and developing campaigns. Interested in this Internet advocacy work, he began teaching himself PHP programming (Personal Home Pages), because at the time it was the best way to build advocacy campaigns online. Because he had just worked hard to develop an environmental model for the *Who Killed Puck?* CD, Minowa decided that he could offer his model to other musicians out there with similar ethics. He didn't want to pursue a career in the business end of music—he had never intended to make Earthology a traditional label to put out other bands—but he could help artists and other record labels manufacture earth-friendly CDs. Minowa poured energy into making a website for Earthology Records.

"The internet search engine algorithms then," Minowa explains, "were a bit easier to master, so I was really big into building different types of environmental issue informational pages and getting them to the top of the search engines." He began to be more successful with grant writing because he could show that his projects would land in the top five search results for something like "Great Lakes water quality." When Minowa launched his first Earthology site during Earth Week in 2001, he used that kind of programming know-how to get it to the top of the search engines, and he succeeded. "If someone searched," Minowa recalls, "for 'environmental music' or 'environmentally friendly CD replication' or 'recycle jewel cases,' we would turn up number one." Indie bands can become successful by having an incredibly catchy song that launches a video and millions of YouTube hits and a subsequent career, but that scenario happens to one in a thousand. More often, success comes (if it does) slowly through hard work and serendipity, and Minowa's geek talents would later prove essential for Cloud Cult's survival.

When people did a web search for recycling their own jewel cases, the option that came up was shipping them to Earthology. Very quickly Minowa started receiving thousands of used jewel cases in the mail. At the same time, Earthology was the only web search result for artists looking to manufacture their CDs environmentally, so Minowa heard from bands out of the area. "I started getting a very large number of requests for price quotes," Minowa recalls. "Since we did it all by hand, from hand cleaning the cases, to inserting the recycled album covers, to burning the actual CDs one at a time, it was more costly per unit than a company that had a machine that manufactured brand-new cases and CDs for people. So our price quote, even to break even, chased most artists off. It was the really environmentally committed artists that we worked with at the time." Earthology Records was beginning to have their principles known, beginning in a very small way to influence the environmental practices of the music business. Although Minowa had fee-based services posted on the website, he spent the bulk of his time answering questions from other labels and artists about how they could green their own product lines. Espousing environmental principles is far easier than living them, and putting them at the center of your business is harder yet, but Minowa persevered at a time early in this century when such principles were far less common than they are now.

Reluctant to give up the dream that his music would get discovered, Minowa used Earthology Records as the plate on which he served up his own music. He made available there *The Shade Project, Who Killed Puck?,* and *Dream Music (for little wizards),* actually posting the albums in a way that made it look like they were all by different artists in order to give the Earthology label the appearance of being something bigger than it was. When 2002 began, Minowa was almost thirty years old. He had made three solo albums. He had started a record label and built a website for the label. But if musical success is measured by having an audience or making money, he had accomplished nothing. What finally launched his music career was the shattering of his personal life and the subsequent tragic upheaval.

From tragedy, Art

Although Craig and Connie enjoyed living in Duluth, in fall 2001 they began looking at rural property, wanting to buy a small farm for several enterprises that they would call Earthology Institute. They would grow organic herbs and cash crops for farmers markets; the institute would be a rural learning center with classes on sustainability and farming; they would build a recording studio, hoping to pull in bands from the Twin Cities and Duluth for recording. They found a farm they liked near Sandstone, Minnesota. The property wasn't the classic midwestern farm of cornfields, rolling pasture, a stock pond, and a red barn, but the farm suited the Minowas. The farmhouse was old but could be remodeled; the small number of tillable acres would be adequate for the organic farming they had in mind. They decided to make an offer.

In February 2002, Kaidin, their two-year-old, much-loved son, died suddenly from unknown causes. With the death, says Craig, "everything totally fell apart." Adding confusion to loss, Connie and Craig had their offer on the Sandstone farm accepted the day that Kaidin died. Their first thought was they couldn't move, but Clarice Richardson urged them to follow through with their original plans, which were made with reflection and care. Grieving deeply, the Minowas moved to the farm.

The old farmhouse needed updating, and Craig and Connie decided to do everything as environmentally purposeful as they could, even if the initial costs were higher. They installed geothermal heating. In the basement, Craig built a music studio out of all recycled or reused materials: he padded his walls with pieces of an old chicken coop and an old toolshed and with old egg cartons; the boards were made out of recycled newspapers; the thickest padding was layers and layers of discarded carpets. The studio, Craig says, was "literally made out of garbage." The Minowas had hoped that buying the farm and growing Earthology into more than a record label would be a new chapter in their lives. But though they tried to throw their energies into plans for the future and tried to make a home without Kaidin, they couldn't manage as a couple.

Grieving differently, the Minowas split up. Connie went off to northern Minnesota to isolate herself in nature. Living in the woods in an off-the-grid, solar-powered cabin, she studied, painted, and wrote. "Like Craig," she recalls, "I tried desperately to find meaning in life. I spent a great deal of time connecting with 'energies that be' and nature." Craig holed himself up in his studio.

Minowa recalls sitting there for days and nights, listening over and over to tapes he had made of Kaidin, and plunking on the piano while he listened: "You know, in there I was totally with him. It was like there was no separation. And I had no desire to go out into the real world where there was a separation." During the next months, Minowa wrote over a hundred songs that expressed the pain of his loss. In his studio writing and recording songs, he had control and could escape. But, he acknowledges now, the obsession became severe. "I was completely insane," he says. "There was no reality outside of the music." Friends and family became worried about him, thinking he might become suicidal.

During this time Minowa continued as best he could his work for the Organic Consumers Association, which he could do from home. Plans for the Earthology Institute fell by the wayside. Minowa recorded a couple of musical acts but realized he didn't enjoy it. He held some public meetings to discuss the possibility of turning the farm into a sustainable community living area, and a few people got involved and started working the land, but Minowa became aware that he was spending his time in the basement music studio. "I discovered," he says, "that I was way too much of a hermit to want to live in a community setting." The farm became largely a hideout. One person who Minowa didn't try to hide from was his old friend Scott West, who was living in Milwaukee and working as the creative director for an apparel company. West began driving nearly every weekend to the new farm, which Minowa was now living on by himself.

"Craig was someone else after Kaidin's passing," West recalls. "He even looked different. I spent a lot of time going back and forth because I was concerned about his well-being." During 2002, when Minowa was writing all the songs, he'd share them with West when they were together. Sometimes Minowa would play the piano, and West would play the guitar or drums, and they'd just beat things around. "At that time," West says, "Craig didn't think he was going to make an album. That's not what he was doing—he was just writing a bunch of songs. He'd share them with me, perhaps as a reality check. And the music was insane and beautiful all at once. He took all that grief and anger and incomprehension and turned it into art, into amazing songs that were bitter and funny and beautiful. He just kept writing song after song. It was like an addiction of writing and recording."

Sarah Young, Minowa's old bandmate from Fable, came to the farm and recorded cello parts on some of the songs, and Minowa got Dan Greenwood, a high-school friend, to visit and play drums on various tracks. West pushed Minowa to take the songs, all those outpourings of emotions, and shape them into an album. "I could hear," West says, "that the music was everything that he needed to heal and to grow. . . . And the music was absolutely brilliant and totally crazy. It's a great picture of exactly what was going on at that point." Young remembers going up to the farm, sitting outside, and hearing the set of songs straight through that would become *They Live on the Sun.* "It was incredible," she says. "But listening to these songs, one after another, I was thinking 'oh my god, he's going crazy.'"

Leaving behind his persona in *Who Killed Puck?* of the artist as environmentalist prophet, Minowa wrote songs in response to Kaidin's death that demonstrate how personal tragedy can send a person into solipsistic despair so deep and terrifying that the world's environmental issues, such as unsafe drinking water or climate change, simply don't matter. Singing in "Toys in the Attic" that he's now alone and no one would believe that he once was married and had a baby, he asks directly, "Hey God . . . / Have I gone crazy?" Gone in *They Live on the Sun* are the principled environmental, anticonsumerism themes. Here, instead, are angry exclamations, short outbursts, songs that fuse a poetics of compression and dream imagery with a music at times tender and pretty but more often dissonant and loud. "Yeah, Craig was crazy," says Greenwood, "but I think that's why that album was so good."

The first song, "On the Sun," begins with a high-pitched synthesizer beeping, which is soon joined by an acoustic guitar and a computerized voice saying something unintelligible. A cello then introduces the song's main melody, and to this backdrop Minowa sings, "We're all made of galaxies and weeds." With no particular story or situation, the song's lyric of only six lines evokes rather than describes. Galaxies, we might say, are beautiful in large part because they are infinite and incomprehensible; weeds are the wild things we don't want in our gardens or yards.

Humans might be made up of both of these, but Minowa doesn't explain how or why. Saying that his grandparents left "this world" to live "somewhere on the sun," he concludes with the lines "I want to leave this world together / And you and I will live up on the sun." Perhaps the "you" is Connie, but it's easy to hear this song as a longing for death, for his joining Kaidin. The music here fuses the two-worlds dichotomy, with the earthbound cello layered under the space-like noises, both being driven forward by drums and acoustic guitar.

The song "Radio Fodder" at one level simply critiques how songs are created in order to get them on the radio. Written for an unknown you, the song starts, Minowa says, "soft and sweet." Later, he sings that the song has gotten quieter, sings that he's gotten mellow in the third verse in order to build to the final chorus. "You like it," he says, "This is our song," and his send-up of pop conventions could be just witty and humorous. But singing "You just want me to sound like every goddamn man on the radio," he almost yells his reaction to this kind of song: "I hate it, I can't breathe / I can't write / I can't live my life like this." His assertion that his life isn't a pop song, either in lyric or construction of verse and chorus, ends with his yelling four times "this is my song" and three times saying "walk" before the song ends in midyell. Bitter and angry he breaks off, as if this is the only appropriate response to life at this moment.

The album's songs have few verse and chorus constructions, nor are the songs catchy tunes with anything resembling a hook. Some are angry outbursts of noise, barely comprehensible, nearly unlistenable. In the ultrafast and dissonant "Turtle Shell," Minowa articulates how he's getting through each day ("This is my turtle shell / I wear it to protect / You cannot hurt me that way") but screams out "turtle shell" repeatedly in a way that is deeply unsettling, suggesting that he needs more and thicker psychological armor. Minowa shapes the classic children's song "Shortenin' Bread" with its upbeat words and melody into something off tune and a bit sinister, the lyric changing to "Somewhere in the deer herd the Unicorn is waking / Licking off its wounds and lifting its head." In the song "Fairy Tale" he twists together numerous famous stories in a bizarre way, with the usual fairy tale ending turned here into a moment of loss and despair.

The songs on the whole are wildly imagistic, confounding if intellectually interesting, evocative even if elusive at the level of intentional meaning. In "Love Will Live Forever," Minowa sings in one verse that the "you" is made of river driftwood, made of water vapor in a second, only to say that underneath your skin are two feathered wings. He concludes his lyric by saying you change like a volcano and your body is just a moment. In "Moon's Thoughts," the narrator says that his insides fell out, and he was surprised at what he saw: "A little boy with dolphin fins, a bucket of Legos and gin / An atomic bomb, the Dali Lama." At times, this bombardment of images leads toward overtly religious references, as in "Moon's Thoughts" when Minowa follows the line "We are Buddha, Confucius, and Jesus Christ," with "But if we want to fly, we've got to leave our shit on the ground / Or is that too much to sacrifice?" Likewise, in "It," the images build toward a questioning of and anger about faith and religion. On this album he works out his grieving before our ears.

When Kaidin was alive, Minowa had discovered, while playing music in his basement studio, that Kaidin was drawn to the microphone. Minowa had recorded his toddler son talking and singing, and during his time of acute grieving he would play the recordings he had made of Kaidin and feel his son's presence. "I would just sit here and play him," he says, "for days and nights." Some of *They Live on the Sun's* strongest songs, more shapely in lyric and music—and the ones where he seems not to be simply venting but processing his grieving—occur near the end of the album when Minowa splices Kaidin into the song. In "Took You for Granted," for example, the arrangement features acoustic guitar, a simple drumbeat, a cello line, and Kaidin talking, which Minowa inserts into the verse breaks. He sings, "I could see all the Universe inside you / You had eyes made of candles / And your body was a medicine bag / That all the world could heal from." He took his son for granted, he says, and in the middle of the song he all but breaks down, crying "I miss you" again and again. But near the end, the cello comes in making the song prettier, and Kaidin is heard singing, and Minowa says, "you were singing" and sounds happy.

In the months after Kaidin's death, having given up on "any kind of God altogether," Minowa delved deep into science and quantum physics, hoping that hard science and rationality might serve him as an antidote to philosophy, religion, or psychology—or even just to feeling too much. "I found magic," he says about his science studies at the time, "in the idea that all living things are made of carbon. There's only one place in the universe that carbon is made, and that is in the belly of a star. So we're all born of a sun, and we are all made of a sun, and our lives are sustained by what the sun feeds us. Our current Sun is in its midlife, but in five billion years, it will begin to expand into a red giant. It will actually swallow the entire Earth and eventually collapse back into itself and become a very dense and small object. So everything on this planet will be back in the belly of the sun. Point being, my philosophy adhered very close to astronomical physics, and I felt comfort in thinking about how Kaidin and I (and all my other loved ones) would be in one place together again." When such big ideas are constructed into art, they can lead eventually to new understanding, as in the song "Your Love Will Live Forever," which Minowa has described as the album's big breakthrough, focusing as it does on "the idea encapsulated in the first law of thermodynamics, which states that energy created cannot be destroyed. So all the love Kaidin had and all of the energy of his every moment continues to resonate in the universe in some way."

Minowa is very smart and well read, and his intellectual nature often serves him well, but at this point in his life rational, intellectual thinking could serve him only temporarily and not deeply. Perhaps he felt comfort in believing that he and all his loved ones would be together, but since that event will take place in billions of years, the comfort is mostly metaphorical. That doesn't mean the comfort isn't occasionally real, but the song that expresses the album's tone and themes most vividly comes not from intellectual explorations in science but from personal grappling with unimaginable heartbreak. In the deeply moving "Sleeping Days, P. II," Minowa sings the following lyric in a vulnerable and often cracking voice over his solo piano, which seems slightly out of tune:

> I hope you awoke to fireworks in the arms of a grass-
> stained wizard.
> Because I can't bear to think that you are gone.
> And somewhere in my belly my little boy is running,
> With unicorns and Elmo and one of Daddy's songs.
>
> Good morning, Baby. Why are you still sleeping?
> You're a plastic boy on a plastic bed. Why didn't they
> take me instead?
> And I like to think you're sleeping in a safe little blue-
> bird's nest.
> And I'll protect your memories with the dragons in my
> chest.

Good night, Baby. Daddy's going crazy.
I'm choking on my sleeping pills, and hanging from a
   window sill.
And I like to think you're dressed up in the beads that
   Momma made.
Will you be there waiting when they take my skin away?

I'm awake for sleeping days. I'm awake for sleeping
   days.

When Minowa sings "Good morning, Baby. Why are you still sleeping?" we recognize, if we know his story, an autobiographical moment of horror, his discovery of his dead son. The song, alternating between moments of artistry and moments of desperation, is an outburst of sorrow coming from deep depression.

They Live on the Sun was obviously not made for commercial radio, which is dominated by the connections and money of the big labels, who pay to have their music on commercial radio stations. Commercial radio works something like this: big-budget labels, shrunk by 2003 through mergers and consolidations to the "Big 5" (EMI, Sony Music, BMG Music, Warner Music Group, and Universal Music Group), pay "independent music producers" to get airtime for their label's artists on radio stations owned by only a few corporations, Clear Channel being the largest. On those stations disc jockeys are told what to play, because commercial radio's goal is to create narrow demographics to help advertisers know to whom they are pitching their wares. A very small sample of music being made is ever played on commercial stations, so if you're an obscure band on an unknown label, you don't even bother trying to play that game.

With only a tiny promotional budget, Minowa hired the Planetary Group, a boutique artist development firm, founded by Chris Davis and Adam Lewis, that is willing to create specific radio campaigns for a new band. *They Live on the Sun* went out to nearly four hundred college radio stations. "We did college radio for Cloud Cult," recalls Lewis. "And the band just really struck a chord from day one when we sent it out. The songs were incredibly strong." The role of college radio stations for bands with little money cannot be overestimated. For an unknown band, time and effort can replace money as the sole reason for getting played. After the initial mailing went out from the Planetary Group with the CD and promotional materials, Minowa made numerous calls to music directors at the college stations, first, to ask if they had received the CD, and then, in a follow-up call, whether they had listened to it and were adding the album to their station's playlist.

These calls to music directors were necessary. Getting the CD added to a station's collection means that the individual deejays will listen and decide if they want to spin the record. At that point, the music itself, not the business of the music industry, becomes crucial, because if the deejays like the album and play it, and listeners call in and request songs, the album will get spins, which the station records. And each station, each week, sends its top thirty songs to the *College Music Journal,* commonly called *CMJ.*

The subheading for *CMJ* is "New Music First," and as a music events/publishing company, *CMJ* is greatly influential. They host the CMJ Music Marathon every fall in New York, which showcases new bands on the rise, and their website is filled with reviews, interviews, and announcements of tours. But perhaps their most important task is gathering, tabulating, and then reporting what songs are actually being played on college and noncommercial radio—*CMJ* publishes the "Top 200" charts for each week. If a band is slowly building a fan base among young people, that rise will be noticed on the *CMJ* charts.

College radio stations, of course, don't play music only by obscure bands on minor labels. College radio helped break the careers of R.E.M. and U2 in the 1980s, when they were signed by major labels but weren't getting the push to land them consistently on commercial radio. And undoubtedly college students frequently play Dylan or the Beatles, as well as jazz, songs from musicals, and the like. But they do attempt to play the music that the industry has disregarded. Carleton College, in Minnesota, has a station that exemplifies this position. KRLX always makes the top ten lists of college radio stations, and two of their music directors, Karl Snyder and Keagon Voyce, say that they "strive to be the antithesis of commercial radio." Not only does every CD that comes to them get heard, but a staff member writes several sentences about the album, recommends a few songs to play, and then uploads the music to the station's computer. The student deejays, no matter the theme or musical genres of their show, have to play at least one song off the week's "new" list for every hour they're on the air. It's possible that for some of these shows only a dozen or so people may be listening, but at least someone is hearing the band's music, and if this is happening in college stations across the country, a fan base can be built slowly if people like what they are hearing.

With Minowa acting as his own obsessive publicist, asking college radio station music directors to take note of his album, pushing the label's environmental principles, *They Live on the Sun* charted on *CMJ*'s Top 200 list. In the documentary *No One Said It Would Be Easy,* Minowa tells the story of getting a phone call from the music radio director at an Alaskan university, who asked him if he was sitting down. When Minowa asked why, the director said, "because your album just went to number one on our station." Other stations called: the album had gone to number two in Denver, and number one at Radio K, the station of the University of Minnesota.

What were these college students hearing and then responding to? Why were they playing an album difficult to listen to by a band they had never heard of? There's no radio tracking of particular songs, as there is with commercial radio and *Billboard* charts, and so it's not known which songs were getting played. But a possible answer emerges from comments by Ian Anderson, who founded the indie label Afternoon Records when he was eighteen. Head of the Minneapolis band Aneuretical, Anderson recalls hearing *They Live on the Sun* and reading about Minowa's personal life: "I thought, here's the real emo. The music being peddled then as emo, where someone's sad because their girlfriend split and they can't find a job, that just seemed trivial compared to what we were hearing from Cloud Cult."

If the college stations were playing his record, someone was listening, which, Minowa says, made him happy to know. But the most important listener, it turned out, was Minowa himself. "I remember getting in the car one day," he says, "and hearing a song from the album on the radio for the first time. . . . It was like an extreme reality of being in this horrible dark space, and working through all this grieving, and all of a sudden hearing a song on the radio with Kaidin's voice in it. And I realized that he's going up through the radio waves right now." And then came the big realization: "Every moment that we lived together was energy and light that goes through the universe. . . . His going through the radio waves and being all over out there made it all sink in, made me feel that I wanted him all over the universe, I wanted him alive everywhere. . . . It was a way of bringing him back to life in the real world. I knew he was alive here in the studio, because I was with him all the time, could have his spirit come and be with me in this space, but out there I couldn't, and then all of a sudden I could, like he's there!"

After Kaidin's death, Minowa did not follow Elisabeth Kübler-Ross's "stage-model" formulation of how people move through profound loss, from denial to acceptance along a path of anger, depression, panic, guilt, and worry. Nor, of course, did Minowa follow a "medical model" of mourning, which sees grief as a group of symptoms that at some point disappears, aided, perhaps, by antidepressants or an exercise program. Listening to *They Live on the Sun,* many people, including therapists, would likely believe that Minowa was mired in nonacceptance of death. His statements about Kaidin being present in the studio with him and Kaidin being alive going through the airways would suggest to many that he was simply in deep denial. But perhaps not.

At this point in his life, rethinking all his philosophies and beliefs, oftentimes feeling depressed and sometimes near self-admitted insanity, Minowa began a long search that would lead him eventually to believe that there's a material world and a spirit world that are permeable. What we call a human death is a passing into another realm. Perhaps something extraordinary has to happen for a person to see or even sense the spirit world, but that is no reason to deny its existence, Minowa came to believe. He has said that during this time he was feeling strongly that he didn't need an excuse to say there's an afterlife, not an afterlife such as the Islamic paradise or the Christian heaven but rather one right here, on earth. "I just refused," he said, "to accept the fact that I would never be with him [Kaidin] again."

Because of his belief that through music Kaidin could be out there in the world, Minowa came to feel the concert experience as something very spiritual: "I felt like I could bring him back and be with him and that I could share that sort of energy with the audience, too." Minowa's acute stage fright, with him

for ten years no matter what band he had been in, was suddenly lessened. He wanted now to play his music live in order to
bring Kaidin's spirit back. Minowa got Dan Greenwood and Sarah
Young together, and they rehearsed and played a few gigs. *They
Live on the Sun* is an exceptionally layered album, full of ambient noise, multiple odd instruments, and strange shifts in time
and key—a trio of guitar, cello, and drums wasn't going to capture the album's sound. But in a sense, the success or failure of
those concerts was immaterial. Minowa had survived, and he had
a band. Cloud Cult as we now know it had begun.

The psychoanalyst John Bowlby, who wrote a monumental
study of attachment, separation, and loss, has insights into the
mourning process that are useful to understand Minowa's grieving and what happened to him after making *They Live on the Sun.*
After an initial reaction to the loss, Bowlby says, a person usually undergoes a phase when numbness is mixed with moments
of outburst and anger, which then often turns into a yearning
and searching for the lost person. The next phase, Bowlby suggests in *Loss: Sadness and Depression,* is a period of despair that
comes from the griever's sense that the present and future life
has become unscripted. Moving to eventual acceptance of the
loss will come only with a reimagining of one's role and life, and,
indeed, Minowa reconsidered his life because of the album—he
became the songwriter, singer, and front man for an indie rock
band, which he wanted to keep going rather than to break up.

Minowa showed his aspirations by building a website for
Cloud Cult specifically, separate from Earthology, one that would
focus on the band's activities (minimal as they were). The website
went public on December 13, 2003, and included a web store.
Using the strategies he had devised earlier for building environmental advocacy campaigns online, Minowa tried to make the
Cloud Cult website personal and interactive. He took an open

source OS Commerce system and tailored it to his needs, which included releasing MP3 downloads that most bands were telling their fans to go to iTunes for. "The blessing of PHP programming," he recalls, "was that I could create a system where there could be a specific product that would have a specific e-mail response upon purchase, and in that e-mail response, I could create a link to a zip file, and let the web server take care of the rest. And we would keep 100 percent of profits. My biggest problem was server load problems, just because most servers at that time couldn't handle a flow of people coming to download something."

In January 2004, six months after the release of *They Live on the Sun,* Minowa put out a new Cloud Cult album, *Aurora Borealis.* When he hadn't been phoning college radio station managers, he was in his studio writing and recording new songs, trying still to grapple with the meanings of Kaidin's death and his own purpose. The new songs begin to point toward a way through the disabling moments of grieving, but the states of being that Minowa explores are no less transitory. On many of the songs, the "I" is divided or alone, still trying to understand the relation between self and others, self and the world. In the opening song, "Breakfast with My Shadow," Minowa's discussion with his shadow self, an alter ego, leads to an important question: "Can you fall in love with the things you only know / The things you may never touch?" The speaker is less interested in providing answers than asking questions, and he concludes with a second important question, one coming from a dinner conversation with his shadow: "If I truly believe that things can change / Will I wake up to something different?" Philosophers have argued for centuries about the role of the mind in shaping one's reality, and anyone deeply grieving has at some moment wished to assert his or her will and say "enough." But if the mind does have some shaping role so that we aren't passive victims of our circumstances, people mourning know how a hard-won version of reality can easily come undone.

"Breakfast with My Shadow" ends with Minowa asking, "will I wake up to something different?" and the next song, "Alone at a Party in a Ghost Town," suggests that he won't. In a repeated refrain, he says that he's alone at a party in a ghost town, a striking image of someone grieving, particularly because he also sings that "we will get, we will get / what we're deserving." The line could mean that the future holds promise, but in the context of this song where the speaker is alone and alienated, he seems to have gotten what he was deserving, and it isn't good. As an environmental scientist, Minowa intellectually understands life and death in relation to an ecosystem's sustainability, understands that *Homo sapiens* is just one species among many, and so he can write the rather strange line, "There is hope in the worms and the maggots / 'Cause they're breaking it down." But the song's very title and his near-desperate singing, which sounds close to wailing, suggest his raw emotions; worms and maggots contributing to the cycle of life isn't going to be emotionally helpful to the question he sings several times, "Are you there, are you there, anybody?" The song is very fast—hyperkinetic, even—with its whoops and its slamming fuzzed-out guitar that sounds more like Superchunk than Cloud Cult.

Aurora Borealis is fueled by Minowa's grieving over his separation from Connie as well as the death of his son. "You won't find you / Unless you lose your mind / And you let go of all the things you cling to," Minowa sings in "All Together Alone," a song full of desperate assertions countered by contradictions, an assessment that fits much of the record in general. He asks three times, "Have we gone wrong? Or are we growing?" and he vacillates between being "crushed by all this madness" and "exploding from this beauty." Writing in "Chandeliers" that "love scares me," he gives at least a partial reason why: "I'm always dumbing up the smart things / And smarting up the dumb things / And messing up the good things." The sound here is different than the sound of the angry and alienated songs. "Chandeliers" is slower, with more guitar and less synthesizer. And in this song he reaches for images that contrast sharply with being alone in a ghost town. "Did you see the stars last night?" he asks, and then he calls the stars "Punctuation for a perfect poem." In the next stanza, echoing the same melody, he asks "Did you see God last night?"

Minowa is deeply spiritual, a religious person who belongs to no church but questions and seeks understandings of the world as well as human life in relation to all this world. God in this song is both those stars shining in the night sky and "an eighty-year-old on a red tricycle." For Minowa, God is in all things and in the mysteries of our existence. The year he was writing these songs, he recalls in the documentary *No One Said It Would Be Easy,* "there was so much solar activity that almost every night I'd go outside there would be aurora borealis. It just looked like these huge dancing spirits, and I was feeling more and more like I was in touch with Kaidin's energy." While Minowa always felt comfort on his farm in growing things that rooted him to earth, living there also pointed him toward the nighttime sky and cosmic philosophizing. "You look up at the stars every night, the aurora borealis, and you know, it's kind of cliché," he says, "but you understand that there's a huge, massive, unraveling cosmos out there, and that we're tumbling along inside of it. . . . When I write music, I stare off at the stars, and wait, and what often comes out of that process are the big questions: Why do we die? And what should I do on any given day? And why did I get to wake up this morning?"

The songs "Northern Lights" and "The Sparks and Spaces between Your Cells" serve less as songs—with a verse and chorus—than they do as wordless constructs of sound that might accompany our observations of nature, whether the aurora borealis in a night sky or the ocean floor in a deep-sea dive. "Northern Lights" has eerie noises and Kaidin talking in the background. "The Sparks and Spaces between Your Cells," which sounds like something the composer Brian Eno might have written, is full of ambient sounds, some that come from a synthesizer but others that might be short samples of noise found on a computer. The sounds draw you in, as if you're shrinking, diving into your skin, exploring the unseen and unknowable. Minowa doesn't end the album by leaving us with such ambient sounds—he's a believer also in the power of words—but he does tie together in an artful way these songs to the others on the album when in "Lights inside My Head" Minowa follows the observation that he's been seeing lights inside his head with the declaration "I'm not broken." The arc of the album moves from depression to a less alienated emotional state, and he comes to this different place via these ambient nature songs. Hell is the fear of pain, he sings, and heaven is the faith that things will be OK, and at album's close he may be only reaching out for, rather than having, that faith. But he is reaching, nevertheless, and in one of the album's tenderest moments, he sings, "will you love me through these changes?" Having suffered one enormous loss, the death of his son, he doesn't want a second, the end of his marriage and of life as he has known it.

In *Aurora Borealis* Minowa begins to shape his strong emotions more artistically, rather than just venting them, and we see this in part in a song such as "Princess Bride," where over his own music he splices dialogue samples from the movie. The samples are some of the most famous lines in the movie, and Minowa is clearly having fun when he sings background harmonies to "Mawwage is what bwings us togever today" and weaves that with "Throw down your arms, I mean it," all against a driving drumbeat and a beautiful cello line. In the clever song "State of the Union," he rearranges bits of dialogue from speeches by President George W. Bush. "Mr. Speaker," the song's lyric begins, "members of Congress, and fellow citizens. Every year by law and by custom we meet here to threaten the world. The American flag stands for corporate scandals, recessions . . ." When Minowa splices together Bush saying, "our first goal is to show utter contempt for the environment," he follows with a loud outburst of applause, just as approximately half of those attending do with every utterance in any president's State of the Union speech. With a strange set of background melodies and ambient noises and off-rhythm beats, Minowa expresses his anger about environmental and political matters in the United States. But it's not anger or sorrow about what has happened in his life. Neither "Princess Bride" nor "State of the Union" has the usual "I" speaking about his emotions or situation.

Just as the satirical songs built of lyrical samples are one measure of change from *They Live on the Sun* to *Aurora Borealis,* so is Minowa's inclusion of more conventional pop songs about love and dreams. The speaker in "As Long As You're Happy" says to the girl he has a crush on, "I had wanted to take you to prom / In my ice cream truck." But if she doesn't remember him, or if he hasn't meant much to her, that will be OK, "As long as you're happy." The song's pop structure is accented by a prominent cello part, a descending and ascending bass line that promotes a cheery vibe, and a driving rhythm guitar. The most beautiful song on *Aurora Borealis* is also the most hopeful. The lyric and sound of "I Guess This Dream Is for Me" are so stripped-down that the singer is fully revealed without any of the coverings that anger or loudness or clever lyrics can bring:

> Sometimes you've just got to fall, so you can see the
>   bottom,
> Or you'll never know what's holding you up.
> And this life feels like a dream to me, it's beautiful and
>   it's twisted,
> But for right now, I don't want to wake up.
> So I guess this dream is for me.
>
> I'd tell you the truth, but my angle's always changing.
> I'd point the right way, but I don't think there's any
>   such thing.
> I like to think that it really doesn't matter
> Where you're going or where you're from.
> The truth is always moving, and it's always where you're
>   standing,
> We may disagree but no one's wrong.
> So I guess this dream is for me.

Minowa's tender vocals are accompanied by his acoustic guitar played softly: no distortions, ambient sounds, drums, or amplified instruments. Midway through, Sarah Young's cello comes in sweetly, adding harmony to the vocal melody, providing counterpoint to the guitar picking. The listener of this song can only surmise about what has helped Minowa—perhaps simply the passage of time. But perhaps his music and songwriting helped.

In *Trauma and Mastery in Life and Art,* Gilbert J. Rose discusses numerous connections between grieving and artistic processes. Art counteracts denial, he writes, because mastery of past trauma comes from continuing attempts of the imagination to split off some parts of the past while elaborating on and reintegrating others. Creative work, Rose says, builds up and melts down, again and again, oscillating between imagination and reality, making something that takes on its own reality. Writing song after song about his losses and emotions, disguised or direct, Minowa was doing psychological work that could help him reformulate his own life's story.

A measure of the change from one album to the next comes in a comparison of the earlier "Sleeping Days, P. II," to the new album's "Beautiful Boy," songs that are directly about Minowa's intense grieving over Kaidin's passing. Like the earlier song, "Beautiful Boy" features shimmering piano chords and a simple melody underlying Minowa's shaky, vulnerable voice. But whereas Minowa in "Sleeping Days, P. II" seems near-suicidal and the song feels like a call for help, "Beautiful Boy" shows sadness, not depression, and shows not separation and alienation but hope for eventual union.

The version of the song on *Aurora Borealis* is a live performance on Radio K, the University of Minnesota public radio station. Because radio waves penetrate very deeply into space, Minowa felt that the performance was like having the most powerful megaphone in his hands through which he could talk to Kaidin. "I was living alone at the farm then," he recalls, "and I just played recordings of him constantly in the background and wrote this song to him. I stayed up all night just doing it over and over, and then I hit the radio station. When they gave me the microphone and piano, I had a cassette player next to me with a tape of him talking on it, and I put it on and instantly felt like the radio tower was a direct bridge between me and him, and I sang in a way I never had before, and I honestly 100 percent felt like I had him back with me. It was a very clear indicator that if I could do that more frequently, including on stage, I could get in direct contact with him. So that album ended with me having a new 'bridge' to the afterlife that I was very excited about."

The song begins with Kaidin talking and saying "Daddy," and then the piano enters, followed by Minowa singing, "I'm climbing to the sun on a cobweb made of tinkertoys." Minowa asks three times in the first chorus, "Where did you go?" as he makes his climb. In the next verse, halfway there, he sings, "There are ghosts all around me / And I see your face in the sun." By the last verse, the speaker has reached the sun, saying to Kaidin, "you are beautiful" and "I'm so tired." The song closes with Minowa singing again, three times, "Where did you go?" before closing with the line, "Beautiful, beautiful boy."

Many people are uncomfortable with strong emotions expressed directly, and for listeners who know the story, "Beautiful Boy" might be difficult to hear. This singer/writer simply loved too deeply, and while we're used to pop music describing grand loves that end between two teenagers or two adults, hearing love of a parent for a child that literally, not figuratively, ends in death is heartbreaking. But it's not like listening to a singer who you suspect is descending into drug addiction or madness. This is like listening to someone moving past our common cultural ways of understanding the world. In his late eighteenth-century work *The Marriage of Heaven and Hell* William Blake wrote, in lines that caught the attention of one Los Angeles band in the 1960s: "If the doors of perception were cleansed every thing would appear to man as it is, Infinite. For man has closed himself up, till he sees all things thro' narrow chinks of his cavern." Blake and many artists since have emphasized the human imagination's transformative power, which arises when something powerful happens that shifts the person away from society's desires for conformity and emphasis on the material. Such trial or suffering leads the mind and the soul—the creative imagination—to an angle unseen by the conformist or the materialist. The art that springs from this creative imagination then teaches other humans how to live intensely, how to feel deeply, how to understand anew.

As with *They Live on the Sun*, Minowa decided to promote *Aurora Borealis* with college radio stations, and it charted even better. College deejays liked "Princess Bride" and "State of the

Union," as well as the more conventional songs. Adam Lewis from the Planetary Group, who was handling promotion, says that Cloud Cult's success has been due in part to its steady stream of releases: "they were able to come back in short order with more great music." Recognition slowly began to roll in. A few music bloggers plugged the album on their sites. The international online magazine of cultural criticism *PopMatters* favorably reviewed the album. The Minnesota Music Awards nominated Cloud Cult (along with Prince and Paul Westerberg) as one of three "Artists of the Year." And Seattle's prestigious independent radio station KEXP and their influential deejay John Richards began promoting the band.

KEXP deejays choose their own music and aren't beholden to major labels; the station has its own live studio and can bring in any touring band they admire; they promote bands on their Internet site and publicize local concerts; in 2000 they were the first station to offer audio on the Internet 24/7. "KEXP has a major impact on bands and their success," Richards says. "We see it all the time. Recently, bands we discovered or championed early have gone on to popularity, such as Of Monsters and Men, the Lumineers, and Alabama Shakes . . . and in the past we have helped break bands like Vampire Weekend, The National, M83, and Sigur Ros. Going way back we were the first ever to play Nirvana. A station like ours not only takes chances, but it also has credibility as a tastemaker." Because the station is noncommercial, it reports to, and therefore also has influence on, the *CMJ* music charts.

Richards says that he was first simply attracted to Cloud Cult's "amazing music" and then after to the compelling personal story. Asked about his part in making Cloud Cult known in Seattle, Richards replied that "my role was to play them early and often. Introduce them to a worldwide audience and get behind the songs. We also booked them for live sessions and KEXP events

early to get people to see what a great live band they were. We
continue to champion the band in these ways." Adrian Young,
Cloud Cult's longtime manager, says that the band was probably
more popular in Seattle early on than it was even in Minneapolis,
and this was due largely to KEXP. Minowa recalls Seattle as one
of the few cities in the early days where there was a consistent,
supportive fan base: "In fact, I remember doing 'Transistor Radio'
there live for the first time [in 2005], and we were blown away
that this packed venue was totally and completely quiet throughout the entire song. Most other venues on that tour, as soon as
you started performing something quiet, like that song, people in
the bar would see it as a good time to resume their conversations,
so you often could barely hear yourself play."

With *Aurora Borealis* Minowa decided to expand the live
show and make it bigger than the unamplified three-piece that
he had tried in support of *They Live on the Sun,* so he brought
in Mara Stemm on bass. He also wanted to involve the audience
in various ways, and he invited dancers and videographers to be
on stage during songs, though that didn't work out. Having a
painter on stage met with more success, developing eventually
into a Cloud Cult staple—Connie painted for a concert in Duluth,
and Scott West for some regional concerts. With the growing
local excitement about the band, Minowa decided to have Cloud
Cult do its first national tour, beginning in Texas and then moving
through the Southeast.

The impetus to head south came from radio charting and
the desire to perform at the South by Southwest (SXSW) music
festival in Austin, Texas, which by 2004 had become the place
for unknown bands to be discovered by the national press, by
influential bloggers, or even by A&R reps from labels. But when
Cloud Cult was nearing Austin, they discovered that their SXSW
slot wasn't advertised in the program and was a makeshift setup

under a bridge. Unhappy about such a situation, they changed course when a festival organizer who was a fan of the song "State of the Union" asked Cloud Cult to play at a protest planned at President Bush's ranch in Crawford. On March 20, Cloud Cult performed with black helicopters flying overhead and was followed on stage—which was really just a field—by Ralph Nader. Minowa remembers the band feeling way out of its league.

After the protest, Cloud Cult headed to New Orleans, through Mississippi, to Atlanta, and then north from there. The tour's schedule was largely based on radio charting. *Aurora Borealis* had gone to number one on college radio in Athens, Georgia, and was in the top five in Atlanta and Hattiesburg, Mississippi. Band members believed that if they were getting good college radio play, they would have a good turnout, which turned out not to be the case. "You know," Minowa recalls, laughing now, "nobody came to the shows."

A band without a radio hit has to pay its dues, just get out there and be heard, even if by few people. The social media that indie bands now use to get attention was just beginning to emerge: in 2003 Myspace was launched, but Cloud Cult didn't yet have a site; YouTube was still a year away; Facebook wouldn't be available for everyone until 2006. All Cloud Cult hoped for on this tour was to have someone attend the concerts, and a night when they sold a couple of CDs helped pay for some gas or food. Dan Greenwood remembers playing in New Orleans "in front of nobody except for my two friends, Adam and Jackson."

If you're trying to make money or become known, such touring is frustrating at best. But Sarah Young believes that although it was disappointing that so few people saw the band perform, the band members were "really trying to get the music to do something." Greenwood actually remembers it as a blast, because there were no expectations. "It was like we were touring for touring's sake," he says, "not out to prove anything, just out to share our music. I remember playing in Hattiesburg in front of ten people, and it was awesome. You can meet people. You can talk to people, like it was a personal thing." A band with little money needs help, and Cloud Cult often found such help along the road, with people offering to let them sleep on couches or providing a meal. One of the ten people who attended the Hattiesburg concert was Brigette Hutchison, who later contacted them and volunteered to be the merchandise person for the Happy Hippo tour. And on this tour, and ones to come, Cloud Cult had the willing hands of Adrian Young, Sarah's husband.

Adrian began dating Sarah in 2003, and when he found out that she played cello in an indie rock band, he was worried because he was afraid he wouldn't like its music. Adrian exemplifies Minnesota Nice in its best sense, and so perhaps it's a surprise that he could become a successful manager in what is usually thought of as a cutthroat business. Before meeting Sarah, he had no experience with bands or as a manager. He began just by helping with mailings, helping get CDs ready to sell at shows, and working the merchandise table. "I kept helping out because of Sarah and because it was fun and I believed in the music. And then I helped more, and at some point, right before *The Meaning of 8* came out, I became officially the band's manager, which they hadn't had before." Like others then and to follow, Young saw something in Cloud Cult that went beyond entertainment. Asked why he was willing to put so much time, energy, and money into helping Cloud Cult be successful, he mentions the band's principles: "Cloud Cult had a purpose, dealing with grief and loss, and also getting bands and people to lead a more sustainable lifestyle. I often didn't feel proud about the company I was working for, who gave me a paycheck, but I could feel great about Cloud Cult."

Few people came to the shows, so the live gate didn't pay

the bills, but Minowa did learn more about how songs that he wrote for an album could or could not be played in concert. "I had two different recording styles going on from *Aurora Borealis* to *The Meaning of 8*," he says. "Some of the early songs are just me in the studio doing as much layering as I want to, without any intention of ever doing the song live, and some of the songs are performed and recorded as a four-piece. So during this stage in the live shows, there were a limited number of songs from the albums that we could do live. I was doing guitar and keyboard at the time, so I did a lot of triggering samples to try to bring some of the more electronic elements to the palette on stage, but many of the Cloud Cult songs have so many tracks going at the same time, that even triggering samples here and there didn't fill that electronic space. The overall live show was much more restricted back then, and I often felt like we were performing covers of Cloud Cult songs just because the live product sounded so different from the albums. Having said that, the band was all very talented and dedicated, and we did our best to make things happen on our extremely limited budget."

The opening scenes of John Burgess's Cloud Cult documentary, *No One Said It Would Be Easy,* show the Minowas on their small organic farm, harvesting vegetables. The farm, Minowa says, is a sanctuary where "all the ideas are born, where all the peace comes from, and where we can center ourselves." And it's where he returned after his *Aurora Borealis* tour to write more songs, to record them in his studio, to try to make ends meet with various part-time jobs. Although the tour was discouraging because it demonstrated that Cloud Cult's reputation didn't extend outside the upper Midwest, the tour did not refute the gains that the band had made. Cloud Cult would need to maintain momentum by releasing a new album and touring again.

Fans Write

What I love about Cloud Cult's music is how honest it is. Innocent, bizarre, beautiful, and so childlike. It makes me wish I didn't have to grow up, but shows me that adulthood can be bizarre and beautiful, too. It tells me that I'm not the only one who feels scared and small and alone, who wants to feel safe.

—Justin MacDonald, 16, Newtown Square, Pennsylvania

I met my best friend at the age of two in our preschool classroom, and from that moment onward she was the only person who truly understood me. We grew up more like sisters than friends, our close families celebrating everything together from holidays to our birthdays, which were less than a week apart. And then, in the summer before we were to turn twenty-two, she took her own life.

I was well aware that she had been dealing with manic depression and bipolar disorder for years, but the news of her death and how it happened literally sent me falling to my knees in shock and agony. In the days and weeks and months that followed, my life became an all-consuming flurry of misplaced anger, gut-wrenching pain, and endless questions with impossible answers. I asked myself over and over what I could have done differently, what I could have done to save her. I lost myself in grieving and became isolated from everything but the hurt that was what I had instead of her.

During one particularly emotional evening, I went for a drive to try and clear my head. I put my music on shuffle and tried to think about the road, the moon. At some point, my thoughts quieted just long enough for me to hear the words to a song that until then I had barely noticed was playing. I didn't know the song, but it seemed to know me, and suddenly I found myself driving with a bittersweet flood of tears streaming down my face. It was the first time I had felt true understanding for what I lost. It was as though the band, who I would soon learn was Cloud Cult, had somehow found me rather than the other way around.

I bought every other Cloud Cult CD and played them non-stop. I listened, I sang along, I cried, and somewhere along the way I began to heal. Spending time absorbing the lyrics and the messages within them became an incredibly effective form of therapy. It helped me to accept the fact that I will never understand why things happened the way that they did, and to decide that it is important to continue living my own life anyway. It helped me realize that there is energy in everyone, energy that can never be destroyed, and therefore parts of my best friend will always be here even if her physical body isn't. It taught me that pain can be used to create beautiful things that may then find others and help pull them from their own turmoil.

Now, when asked why Cloud Cult is my favorite band, my answer is simple: They helped me understand that the death of my best friend didn't have to kill me, too; and though I may never be fully healed, that's okay. I still have energy in me.

—Stacy Shearer, 26, Los Angeles, California

I tend to get a little tongue-tied in trying to describe how and why I love Cloud Cult so deeply. It might have something to do with the fact that Cloud Cult's music doesn't make me think, it makes me feel. Listening to them is not an intellectual experience; it's an emotional and spiritual one.

I feel like we (humans) often talk above or beneath or around what really is asking to be talked about. We're obsessed with trivialities, likes/dislikes, drowning in opinions, and it all seems to be a massive distraction from what's really going on, namely: Why are we alive? How best to use our time here? Is there a God? How are we to live knowing we're going to die? Why do we suffer? etc. Cloud Cult marches right up into the face of these questions with an unblinking courage that is bracing. The canvas they're painting on (an appropriate metaphor if you've seen them play live) is cosmically huge.

We've done exhaustive research into the misery of the world and what wretched creatures we human beings are, but far less research into the no-less-greater truth of how wonderful, resilient, kind, and loving we can be. Or could be, given a reori-entation toward the world and ourselves. Cloud Cult's music is aspirational, in the best sense of the word, without ever being moralizing, fussy, or finger-pointing. Each song, in its own way, functions as a kind of optimist's anthem. And Craig's optimism can be trusted because it has been hard-won.

Listening to Cloud Cult continues to inspire me: the band has set a tone for the kind of art I wish to create. They're a carbon-neutral band in a carbon-saturated world, and a heart-centered band in a heartbroken world. I love them dearly, and I'm intensely grateful that Cloud Cult exists.

—Josh Radnor, 38, Los Angeles, California

To me, Cloud Cult embodies empowerment, the interconnected-ness of life, and the beauty and complexity of love. I don't con-sider myself very religious, but every time I've seen the band live, the experience has been transcendent and made me think about how miniscule and seemingly insignificant we are on this earth, and yet how that makes our existence that much more unique and powerful because we are all we have.

—Alicia Hlebain, 22, Minneapolis, Minnesota

Like Craig and Connie, my wife and I have also suffered through the loss of a child and have been to the brink of what should have been the end of us as a couple. But also like those two, we are somehow stronger today than we were then. We also have since had another beautiful, healthy little boy. Through it all Cloud Cult has been my musical inspiration and foundation. They have gotten me through some very rough storms and have always had that "lighthouse" effect for me. It was quite literally love at first "sound" the first time I heard them.

They are the one band that can run the entire gamut of emotions for me. I can laugh, cry, get anxious, get relief, feel hopeless, or feel grateful. The music is not always happy and positive, but as anyone who has started the journey—neither is life. Cloud Cult is also the only band that is universally accepted in my house. My twenty-year-old son, my ten-year-old son, and my wife all love them, too. (As will the two-year-old, eventually.) A live Cloud Cult show is like church for me, or at least it is what church ought to be, spiritually and emotionally uplifting. So much so, that my ten-year-old son can say that his very *first* concert was Cloud Cult at Orchestra Hall in 2011. We should all be so lucky.

—Jeff Morin, 39, St. Paul, Minnesota

What does Cloud Cult's music mean to me? Love. Their music is the pure, unadulterated outpouring of love. My entire life I have had trouble figuring out what love was and what it felt like. When I first heard Cloud Cult's music, I was captivated. At long last I was able to define love. Not in words but in feelings and sounds. All of their songs, in one way or another, feed on this concept of love. The sad songs dealing with loss convey to me the feelings of a heart shattered and the way we cope. The happy songs convey completeness, wonderment, and exaltation. I have no favorite song. They are all a part of a whole and cannot be separated without destroying the delicate equilibrium the band has in their music. Cloud Cult brings me tears of joy and tears of sorrow. This music has changed my life and, more important, my soul.

—Metgyre Senzig, 28, Milwaukee, Wisconsin

As I skeptically pushed the CD my sister gave me into my truck's CD player, everything before me suddenly melted away. Up until that point, I was a wishy-washy eighth grader with an undefined music taste. My music style blended perfectly with the times. But as "No One Said It Would Be Easy" streamed into my ears, the melodies—so perfectly conducted—went straight to my soul. I had never heard music so beautifully clear and yet so courageously raw. It shattered my philosophy of listening to "popular" music. There was a depth like I had never felt before in music.

As the months went by and my love for this unique band grew, they became my standard for music. If music lacked the lyrical depth and musical magnificence of Cloud Cult, then I threw it out. To this day I have never felt so in tune with a band and what they stand for than I am with Cloud Cult.

—Laura Baker, 21, Tyler, Texas

Cloud Cult, to me, has been a savior. Several years ago I went through a horrible depression, and they helped me get out of it. I listened to their lyrics, wrote them down on little note cards, and taped them to the walls all over my apartment. I read them daily as affirmations that life is good and that life is what you make it. I even wrote a thank-you letter to them for all they had unknowingly done for me, and I got a kind and thoughtful response back.

The positive energy and love that is within every note of their music cuts to my core and makes me a better person. You cannot listen to them without feeling some sort of emotion, usually happiness and joy. You get a sense that no matter what is happening in your life, everything will be okay.

When I listen now, I am reminded to be more loving, to be more patient, to be a better friend, daughter, sibling, teacher, and colleague. I use some of their songs on my exercise mix so they keep me motivated. I sing along at great volume on my ride to work. Their live shows are when I worship, and for a diehard atheist that's saying a lot. Their music is the closest thing I have to religion or spirituality. I *do* think that it's a miracle just to be breathing, and I *do* give thanks to my present day, and I *do* choose to turn it into gold. And Cloud Cult is 100 percent responsible for that.

—Shelley Pecha, 44, St. Paul, Minnesota

I first heard Cloud Cult while streaming The Current online at work. I knew I liked them immediately, because I completely stopped what I was doing so I could give the song my full attention. I could go into detail about how interesting and different their sound is: how they rock a three-piece harmony instead of a two-piece harmony, and how they pull off this added layer of complexity with seeming ease and grace. I could talk about how their lyrics succinctly communicate big, bold, beautiful ideas that enrich and deepen and expand one's view on the world. But what I really want to say about what Cloud Cult's music is that listening to them was like finding a soul mate—someone who simultaneously understands exactly who I am and where I am at in my journey in this world, yet inspires me to do and be more, not out of any archaic notions of what I should be, but in love, telling me what I could be.

I think that's what I love about them the most. No matter what subject they're dealing with, they handle it with love. A sense of love permeates everything about them. Even their darker songs, with subject matters so devastating and crippling that you wonder how they could even create something so beautiful out of it, are just ensconced in love. I think, more than anything, this speaks to their ability to completely embrace the human experience, with all its various hues and flavors.

I know it seems like a long way to get to here (and I don't think Cloud Cult would mind the journey of it), but in summary, the music of Cloud Cult reminds me that I'm human: fragile, weak, strong, full of contradictions and complexity. And it is precisely because I'm human that I am beautiful.

—Alicia Sanchez, 30, Garden Grove, California

June 18, 2012. I was enjoying a picnic with friends at Chicago's Pritzker Pavilion in Millennium Park. That there was a concert was incidental to our gathering; we were friends finding a pleasant place to spend an evening together. The opening act provided agreeable background music as the sun set behind the city skyline. Once Cloud Cult started, though, the atmosphere changed for me. At the risk of seeming rude to my friends, I twice tore myself away from the conversation and moved into the stands to better experience the music. The second time I stayed until the end, mesmerized and moved by this band without fully understanding why. There was something about the songs that was moving me, an emotional content to the lyrics and music that resonated.

I texted my daughter, a college radio deejay and progressive music enthusiast. Her response confirmed that I had stumbled into a "legit" (her term) indie concert on a beautiful summer night in Chicago. I wished my second-born a happy twentieth birthday and let her be jealous for one night. (The next Tuesday night I got a shout-out on her radio show for being at a Cloud Cult concert plus a playing of my requested Cloud Cult song—a thrill of recognition for this often-invisible mother.)

As to why Cloud Cult's music resonated with me, it didn't take long on the Internet to find the answer. It was our tragic connection: the death of a child. The loss of our beautiful shining stars, our sons. It was all there in the music. More than you ever wanted to experience in your lifetime, for sure, yet you'd endure it again given the chance. For love.

Written in loving memory of my first child, my light for twelve and a half glorious years, Beau Charles Benoy. 11/26/88–6/22/01.

—Robin Benoy, 60, Riverside, Illinois

Psychological and Philosophical Sojourns

On March 22, 2005, Cloud Cult released its third album in less than two years, *Advice from the Happy Hippopotamus,* a marked departure from *They Live on the Sun* and *Aurora Borealis.* During the composing of songs for the earlier albums, Minowa was alone on the farm, desperately calling on Kaidin and the spirits to come visit him. By now, after confronting his philosophies about the meaning of life and mortality, he had come to believe that the two states of being we call life and death are less separate than most Western and modern people think, that the boundaries between a material world and a spirit world could be penetrated, particularly through dreams. When he was writing the songs on *Advice from the Happy Hippopotamus,* Minowa says, "I felt like the sleeping dream world was one of the doorways between here and the Other Side, so I used it as much as I could." He began wearing a sleep mask on stage (which he still wears). "It felt ceremonial," he says, "where I could enter the dream world or spirit world before getting on stage, and then could really try to tap into it through the music."

On these new songs Minowa works his personal life less directly and more obliquely and symbolically into the album's subjects. The Happy Hippopotamus is a figure from Minowa's dream journal. Digging through that journal for ideas and images to use for songs, he kept finding material from a hippo. "I had had recurring dreams about this hippopotamus for many years," he says, "and it's weird but in the dreams this hippopotamus comes and I'm just running after it . . . like I'm supposed to follow it. And when I'd wake up, I'd have advice. It never talked to me, but when I'd wake up, I knew there was something that I needed to write down. And so going through the journals, I noticed at one point that half the lyrics I was putting down were from this hippopotamus." In Freud's psychoanalytic theory of selfhood, the unconscious mind contains those anxieties, fears, desires, and memories that are not immediately available to our conscious mind. The unconscious is the keeper of forgotten memories, which may emerge into consciousness at some later time, and unconscious feelings are often expressed symbolically in dreams, which is why processing one's dreams can help people better understand their own motivations and emotions. The Happy Hippopotamus served Minowa as a source of inspiration, perhaps even as the crucial figure that could lead him from *needing* advice for his life to *giving* advice based on his own overcoming of tragedy.

"Take your strong pieces and use them for living," Minowa sings in the opening song, "Living on the Outside of Your Skin," where he suggests that he's ready to be vulnerable and reach out emotionally, rather than erecting psychological defenses. In the beautiful song "What Comes at the End?" he writes, "You'll be a hummingbird / And I'll be a bumblebee / And we will fall in love in our new skin." Though he recognizes that his "skin's still made of memories," which will ensure continuity and struggle, he writes of the desire to begin over in "Start New."

Adopting the hippopotamus as an artistic muse not only helped Minowa psychologically, it also showed him a composing process: "With the Happy Hippo I was starting to realize that I was receiving a lot of medicine in my dreams, and that, in regards to lyric writing, it was increasingly important for me to let go of the lyric writing process and let it be guided by outside forces. I've heard other artists say it before, but it's best to let the messages come from something bigger than the self. If I let Ego get in the way in songwriting (worrying about critics or hipsters), I'll mess it all up. It's best to get to the point that your conscious brain is no longer present. The intention is to symbolically lose myself (no more Craig Minowa) and tap into the dream world. My job is to be an effective conduit." As with many creative endeavors, however, becoming that conduit is mysterious and can't simply be willed.

Songwriting happens for him, Minowa says, when he's doing mundane tasks. He's constantly brewing melodies and lyrics in his head, but he rarely sits down at the piano or with his guitar intending to write a song. He doesn't go to a coffee shop for the afternoon to compose a lyric. The songs often come to him as a whole if he just waits, waits for a set of lyrics or an angle on a subject or a melody and arrangement. He then fleshes out the ideas later in the studio. It's often constraining, Minowa says, to have a specific outcome for a song planned. Those songs usually end up feeling less genuine. The best songs are those that just go where they will, as he attests to in describing the genesis of "Transistor Radio," the touching, wise song about his grandfather: "With 'Transistor Radio' I was on a road trip to Milwaukee to hang out with Scott West. I rarely listen to the radio in the car, because it's the perfect time to write. The longer you can go sitting in a quiet place without distraction, the more you start to hear the music and the words. It's the distractions that make the process take so long. So I just sat in silence for the drive, and 'Transistor' was pretty much done by the time I got home. The story just played itself out. I think that this is the source of pretty much all art. It comes from bigger places, and it's our job, as the artist, to just let the message come out."

And for this album, the message and music indeed came out. *Advice from the Happy Hippopotamus* is Cloud Cult's first great album. In a review for *PopMatters*—a highly regarded international online magazine about popular culture—Michael Franco wrote that *Advice from the Happy Hippopotamus* "is an entrancing album that defies categorization," and he rated it a nine out of ten. Asserting that Minowa makes "an enthralling expression of optimism" out of pain, Franco focuses on how the album creates "a mosaic of sound that compiles bits of memories and places them into a larger, more meaningful, context. True, this album is a challenging listen, but only because something approaching genius is at play here, and the modern ear isn't accustomed to hearing such skill."

A similarly laudatory review ran in an even more influential online magazine. *Pitchfork Media,* usually called simply *Pitchfork,* has been an important tastemaker for indie rock since shortly after its beginnings in 1995. In his *Washington Post* piece "Giving Indie Acts a Plug, or Pulling It," staff writer J. Freedom du Lac describes *Pitchfork* as "the hilariously snarky, oft-elitist, sometimes impenetrable but entertaining and occasionally even enlightening Internet music magazine." Though some musicians and fans become upset by the journalistic license granted *Pitchfork*'s staff writers, who are able to write personally and critically, that quality of heartfelt, deep engagement attracts to the site daily viewers by the hundreds of thousands. *Pitchfork* publishes music news, artist interviews, "best of" lists, and, perhaps most important, album reviews. Rating each album from zero to ten and using tenths, *Pitchfork* writers have played a major role in breaking to a wide audience some of the most influential bands of the past decade. Modest Mouse, Broken Social Scene, Arcade Fire—these bands received significant career boosts with rave album reviews. Marc Hogan begins his review of *Advice from the Happy Hippopotamus* by comparing the album to critically acclaimed and influential records by Modest Mouse, Beck, Radiohead, and Neil

Young. Testifying that he's always been "captivated by bands that find quirky beauty in modest everyday moments," Hogan praises the album's "dizzying sprawl," the way Minowa melds "folk, electronics, Arcade Fire emo, and quasi-hippie hoobajoo." Hogan gave *Advice from the Happy Hippopotamus* a rating of 8.3 out of 10, calling Minowa "an insane genius."

The music blogosphere likewise took note of the album. In a way that was typical then and has been since for Cloud Cult, the band got only a modest amount of attention, but what it did get was deeply passionate. Jeffrey Baum, rating the top albums of 2005 on his New York blog *Central Village,* listed *Advice from the Happy Hippopotamus* at number one, and he accompanied that rating with the following comments: "I have raved and raved about these guys to anyone that would listen from the second I first heard them. I've never met anyone who thought this album was anything short of amazing. . . . They combine the vocals, guitar, strings, and electronic beats all perfectly. The album sprawls over a huge stretch of human emotion, but all the songs keep a universal theme of hope in the face of uncertainty as to why we're all here on earth. Very hippie, but legit. . . . I'm confident in saying that there is not a song on this album that is anything short of a masterpiece. And I mean that as sincerely as anything I've ever written. This is the best album of the last year by a landslide. Anybody with ears is doing themselves a great disservice by not bringing this music into their lives."

The songs on *Advice from the Happy Hippopotamus* explore death and life, work and play, endings and beginnings. Songs range widely in their musical structures as well as their instrumentation. Adopting the hippopotamus to serve as a kind of artistic alter ego, Minowa writes music and lyrics befitting work that comes from dreams and the unconscious mind. The songs are appropriately idiosyncratic, even confounding. "What It Feels Like to Be Alive" is simply Minowa saying to a live audience, "Why don't you show the people of the world that you are alive," and everyone screaming, and then Minowa saying to the crowd, "And even more important, show yourself that you are alive." More screaming and yelling follow. And that's the song. In a totally different vein, a young woman narrates a long near-death experience in "Light at the End of the Tunnel," describing how her life played out before her as a fast old-fashioned movie, and then she got to that bright light and decided in her mind "No, I wanna go back." What marks the album overall is how emotionally sure-footed Minowa seems with these oddball, jumpy songs full of offbeat images. Listening to the album is like visiting a carnival funhouse, where our conventional expectations and responses are surprised, where wacky or distorted constructions of our world show us—like a Gaudí building—a playful whimsicality.

In his book about psychology and music, *Sweet Anticipation,* David Huron says that music compared to most arts is repetitive and has substantial predictability: "Most people find pleasure in what is predictable, though they don't want sameness, which can lead to boredom. So pop or rock songs that feel immediately familiar, because the listener has heard similar songs hundreds of times before, are different enough (by being new) that they meet the need for novelty, but are similar enough to give pleasure." But these Cloud Cult songs don't work by being new yet predictable—in general the songs defy expectation, which is why many people say that the album isn't an easy listen. Minowa's voice is unusual—his high-pitched, sometimes off-tune voice sounds similar to Neil Young or Wayne Coyne from the Flaming Lips—as is his singing style. And the songs aren't constructed as typical rock songs with verse, chorus, predictable chord changes, predictable instrumentation, and the like.

The subjects or developments of those subjects are likewise unpredictable, falling outside the general themes of pop music. In "Happy Hippo," for example, Minowa writes, "I like my happy hippo-pot-a-mus. / She's sleeping under my matt-er-us. / She shows me Jesus at the bottom of a colt 45!" and then resets the famous lyrics of Neil Young that Kurt Cobain referenced in his suicide note, turning "It's better to burn out than to fade away" into "You'd best learn to live while you're alive." In the song "You Got Your Bones to Make a Beat," various band members laugh, wail, talk, and then together sing "dum diddy dum diddy" to accompany lines such as "You got your skin to sing a song you better sing a super swell song so," where Minowa's voice goes up at the end into a kind of trilled whoop. The song is mostly sound, like a children's book with few words and incomplete images that is satisfying because it amuses the child's ear. The song "Clip-Clop" has the following humorous lines sung in a kind of dirge: "Clip-clop happy horse / Giddy-up away from No-No-No / into Yeah-Yeah-Yeah." The fantastical makes its entrance when the boy of "Washed Your Car" tries very hard to impress his object of infatuation: after washing her car and mowing her lawn, and being turned down for a date, he builds her cupboards out of his bones, rakes her leaves with his toes, tills her garden with his nose, though she just keeps saying no. The wit of the song turns on how her refusals not only strengthen his resolve but give him a kind of supernatural power.

Numerous songs address topics other than Minowa's grieving over Kaidin's death, such as the beautiful acoustic guitar pieces "Bobby's Spacesuit" and "Transistor Radio." The album even contains upbeat songs such as the rhythmically bouncy "Lucky Today," where the narrator celebrates being lucky even though he has nothing of value in his pocket—he just feels good. With manipulated beats in addition to drums, with its orchestrations and computer samples providing layers to straightforward rock songs, the sound of *Advice from the Happy Hippopotamus* is like a quirkier version of the Flaming Lips' *The Soft Bulletin* or Radiohead's *Kid A*. While there are still songs about car crashes, death, politics, and depression—the themes that pervade the earlier albums are still there—the overall mood is lighter.

Though Minowa was mostly using his dreams as a bridge between the material world and the spirit world, his personal life serves that bridge on two of the best songs on *Advice from the Happy Hippopotamus*. "We Made Up Your Mind" opens with the rather enigmatic lines, "We made up your mind for you last night / So you can decide that you'll be all right." A listener can only guess who the "we" might be. Friends, family? "They" go on to ask two straightforward questions: "Do you believe in you? Are you ready yet?" The answer comes in the next song, as "We Made Up Your Mind" is followed by the more complex "That Man Jumped out the Window," a song whose meaning turns on interpretation of the pair of lines sung six times: "That man jumped out the window / Come back in the window."

Minowa recalls these two songs coming to him one nightmarish winter evening when reality, imagination, dreams, and a spirit world all fused together: "There were three floors at the farmhouse, and in the back area there was a window at the very top that I would sit at every night and stare at the stars during the winter. One night, I felt a really strong urge to jump out the window. It was part depression and part just wanting to see what the universe would do. I felt like life was so weird and unpredictable that I just wanted to see if I could survive it. Again, I wasn't always in my right mind during those days. I was confident that either I would survive it and prove that I'm supposed to be here right now, or I'd bust my back on the ice below and freeze to death and be with Kaidin again. I got very close to feeling this was a good idea, and that was a moment where I must have gotten really close to the other side, because a rush of lyrics came, which was those two songs. I felt, in that moment, like the spirits were singing it to me. I was weeping as it was all coming out, because it was like the room was full of ghosts singing. I couldn't see them, but it was like they were singing these songs front to back for me, and I was writing it down as fast as I could."

The lyric of "That Man Jumped out the Window" takes up a confluence of "being" in which perception, reality, behavior, and expectation become intermingled into something overwhelming and potentially dangerous:

> It's the thoughts that you feed. It's the habits you need.
> It's the things that you don't think that you're seeing,
> When you're really seeing.
> That man jumped out the window,
> Come back in the window.
> That man jumped out the window,
> Come back in the window.
>
> It's your tongue in my mouth. It's the things that we're
>   too scared to talk about.
> It's the feeling that you're dreaming. (You're not really
>   dreaming.)
> That man jumped out the window,
> Come back in the window.
> That man jumped out the window,
> Come back in the window.
>
> It's the feeling that you're falling,
> But there's a fine line between falling and flying.
> It's the feeling that you've lost it,
> What don't you get? What don't you get?

Any great song may have a particular sonic or lyrical turn that seems simply brilliant inspiration; one such moment comes here when Minowa holds the tension of falling by singing the two lines "It's the feeling that you're falling / But there's a fine line between falling and flying" on the same melodic pitch, only to go up one note when he sings the "ing" of "flying." Our pragmatic culture has difficulty with people who seem crazy, who might be suicidal, or who are visited by spirits. And yet Minowa somehow makes compelling music from his angle that gives him a unique vision.

Personal messages from the spirit world can serve a songwriter's psyche well, but such songs rarely contain the music and lyrics that make for popularity. *Advice from the Happy Hippopotamus* had no single to jump-start radio play, and the band had no publicity machine that a label with a substantial promotional budget provides. But because reviewers and listeners who knew the band tended to be very passionate and enthusiastic, Cloud Cult scheduled an ambitious coast-to-coast tour. Brigette Hutchison, one of the ten audience members in Hattiesburg the year before, helped Minowa put solar panels on the van the night before they set out to play the major markets of Philadelphia, Boston, Washington, D.C., New York City, Detroit, Chicago, Milwaukee, Madison, Minneapolis, Denver, Seattle, Portland, San Francisco, Salt Lake City, Santa Fe, and smaller cities in between. The goal with the tour was to web together the markets where the band had strong college radio charting. And, as with the previous tour, not many people showed up.

Minowa recalls the Happy Hippo tour as a disaster in regards to the number of fans: "I remember being very disappointed night after night by the turnout. All the bills were going on my personal credit card, and I was going under fast. I had to pay band members, hotels, and gas, whether the show paid or not, and most of the shows didn't end up paying. There were many near empty rooms, and that tour was coming on the heels of the *Aurora Borealis* tour, which was also sparsely attended." Because of rising expectations, because Minowa believed that the album and the band should be getting more recognition, the Happy Hippo tour was probably the rock bottom for Cloud Cult. The band had to face that perhaps they would never be able to make a living with music, never be able to generate a fan base outside of a few cities. "*Hippo* was my fourth album," Minowa says, "and I really felt like it needed to be our breaking album, as I was going broke. Many people would say that if you haven't made it by your fourth album, you should hang it up." But he didn't quit.

For someone who had always seemed ambivalent about the music business, Minowa was stubbornly dug in to making it with Cloud Cult as a band. He had ambition. He had pride. He believed in his message and music, and indeed, where the band was getting promotion, audiences did come. KEXP promoted the Seattle show, even doing a live in-studio session with the band the day of the concert. Mary Lucia, deejay for KCMP The Current in the Twin Cities, had the band perform three songs live on July 13, a few days before a concert in Minneapolis, and a few months later on September 15, KEXP cosponsored a live session recorded in New York City with WNYC. And those three markets—Seattle, Minneapolis, and New York—had enthusiastic audiences. Minowa remembers keeping afloat by trying to look at the big picture: "With each album, we'd get a little more radio play, we'd have a few more people coming to the show, and we'd get a little more press. When people did come to a show (and I remember shows where as few as two people showed up), they tended to be very deep into the band."

Most important to the later success of Cloud Cult was when listeners of the albums wrote Minowa an e-mail or attended the live shows and talked to him. "Initially there were people coming," he says, "who had also lost somebody, even some parents came that had lost children. They were coming to the shows and talking about how they got strength from certain songs. I thought 'OK, well maybe there's a purpose to the music then, and if it's helping people then that's a good thing.' Part of the reason I wasn't pursuing music hard-core early on was that I wanted to do something good for the planet—which is why I went into environmental science—I just kind of felt like if you write music, it's probably more selfish than anything. That's what it felt like to me at least. But then for the first time, with these people coming, and getting a lot of fan mail, too, I thought I had a purpose with this music."

Though Minowa was losing money as a musician, this newly found belief in a music career serving a purpose beyond himself suggests a connection to Bowlby's thesis that people move through grieving by slowly rescripting their earlier painful life. The first step necessary for Cloud Cult to tour was Minowa getting over his fear of being on stage, which he had done the previous year by coming to feel that performing songs evoking Kaidin was a spiritual experience. The second step for Cloud Cult occurred when Minowa realized that performing music expressing his own views and emotions was not a selfish act, but something that gave meaning to an audience.

The few people who did attend a concert were responding positively to the stage show, which had evolved from the early efforts to reproduce with a three-piece band the songs from *They Live on the Sun.* On the Happy Hippo tour, Minowa brought the painters on as a regular part of the stage show, first Scott West and then Connie. Why have painters in the band? The most obvious answer was that adding visual arts meant that the band was putting on more of a show. The audience could listen to music and watch art getting made. "Painting during a concert," says West, "shows an audience a process. Some of the young people,

First band: Counterpoint practices in the basement of Jeff DuVernay's house during Craig Minowa's senior year of high school, 1991. *Left to right:* Jeff DuVernay, Scott West, Craig Minowa, Josh Lukkes. Courtesy of Jeff DuVernay.

Fable, the band Minowa assembled after releasing *The Shade Project* (1996). *Left to right:* Paul Ludenia, Craig Minowa,

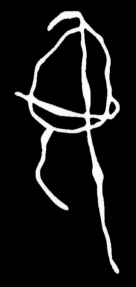

Craig and Connie found this etching by Kaidin on a piece of furniture. It appears on all Cloud Cult releases and promotional materials.

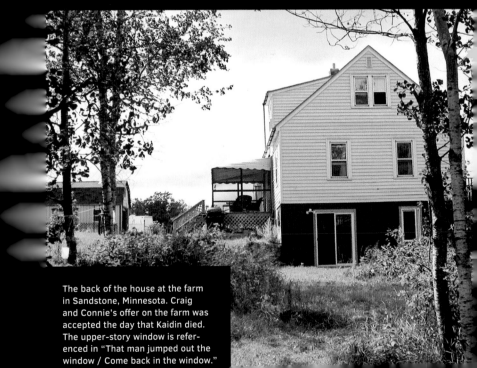

The back of the house at the farm in Sandstone, Minnesota. Craig and Connie's offer on the farm was accepted the day that Kaidin died. The upper-story window is referenced in "That man jumped out the window / Come back in the window."

In the farm's basement
music studio, made
of recycled materials,
Minowa set up his piano
as a shrine to Kaidin.

The first live version of the band Cloud Cult included Dan Greenwood, Craig
Minowa, and Sarah Young. The three played several concert gigs in 2003
after Minowa's acute stage fright had lessened.

Cloud Cult brought Scott West and Connie Minowa aboard as band members—and as onstage painters. A dynamic, visual stage show had evolved. Sarah Young plays cello, Craig Minowa on guitar, circa 2005.

An early gig for the *Aurora Borealis* tour in 2004: Cloud Cult plays at President George W. Bush's Crawford Ranch in protest of the Iraq War. The band would be followed on stage by Ralph Nader. *Left to right:* Sarah Young, bassist Mara Stemm, Craig Minowa, Dan Greenwood.

Craig Minowa at the Republican National Convention, St. Paul, Minnesota, 2008. The officers in riot gear might be wondering if they can keep the peace against this menacing protester.

Cloud Cult on stage at the 2009 Coachella Valley Music and Arts Festival, perhaps the most prestigious festival in the United States. Minowa announced to fans at this concert that Connie was pregnant. Photograph by Stacy Schwartz.

going to charity. Here are the bid board and happy owners of a new painting. Photograph by Stacy Schwartz.

Tours are exhausting, especially when you do all the scheduling, driving, load-ins, and load-outs. Craig Minowa recharges in the green room. Photograph by Cody York.

A sing-along concert moment, circa 2008. "Show the world that you're alive!"

Craig Minowa and Scott West, best friends and in various bands together since high school. West says that Cloud Cult's music influences his painting; Minowa has written songs inspired by West's artwork. Photograph by Cody York.

Shannon Frid-Rubin plays violin. She began with Cloud Cult in 2007 during the *Meaning of 8* tour. Photograph by Cody York.

Rockin' it in concert: Craig Minowa on guitar, Arlen Peiffer on drums, Shawn Neary on bass, and Scott West, painting. Photograph by Stacy Schwartz.

For a small indie band, touring does not mean large motor coaches with bunks to sleep in: Cloud Cult on the road in its biodiesel van, 2010. *Left to right:* Shawn Neary, Arlen Peiffer, Sarah Elhardt-Perbix, and Sarah Young. Photograph by Cody York.

Doing the "Hokey Pokey" in the green room before a show: "Put your whole self in, take your whole self out." Upper left, with glasses, is Adrian Young, longtime helper and band manager from 2007 to 2010. Next to him is Jeff Johnson, who began with Cloud Cult at the 2007 South by Southwest festival, where he worked the sound-board in exchange for a ride to Texas. He has been sound and tour manager since. Photograph by Stacy Schwartz.

Cloud Cult with one of its biggest supporters, Josh Radnor, independent filmmaker and star of the television series *How I Met Your Mother*. Photograph by Cody York.

Connie, Craig, and baby Nova, born in October 2009. "I don't know where we come from, and I don't know where we go / But my arms were made to hold you, so I will never let you go / 'Cause you were born, to change this life."

Cloud Cult at an in-studio session in 2010 at independent music station KEXP, Seattle. Such sessions have been critical in building Cloud Cult's fan base.

Sarah Elhardt-Perbix, hired as a multi-instrumentalist for the band in 2010, plays trumpet during an in-studio session on WNYC's popular public radio music show *Soundcheck*. Cloud Cult has been hosted by John Schaefer for *Soundcheck* three times. Photograph by Cody Yor

Daniel Zamzow, the newest member of Cloud Cult, joined in 2011. Like the other band members, he leads a complicated life of part-time jobs and Cloud Cult tours. Photograph by Cody York.

Publicity shot for the second *Light Chasers* tour, capturing Cloud Cult's blend of cosmic philosophizing and goofiness. Photograph by Cody York.

Publicity shot for *Love.* Photograph by Cody York.

For "Meet Me Where You're Going" on *Love,* Shawn Neary learned the banjo, which he played regularly in the acoustic concerts of 2013 and the hybrid acoustic–electric concerts of 2014. Photograph by Cody York.

Cloud Cult has come far since the days when only a few people might show up for a concert. Photograph by Stacy Schwartz.

In 2009 the Minowas moved to Viroqua, Wisconsin, where their music studio became as large as the great outdoors. Here the band practices songs from the upcoming album *Love*. *Left to right:* Craig Minowa, Shawn Neary, Arlen Peiffer, Daniel Zamzow, Shannon Frid-Rubin, and Sarah Elhardt-Perbix. Photograph by Cody York.

A classic "rock god" photo—a persona Minowa has been reluctant to embrace. Photograph by Cody York.

in particular, know almost nothing about art, and when I talk to them after a concert, they seem to have gotten enthusiastic about painting, at least in the short term." West added another reason for Cloud Cult's innovation: "I think Craig liked having painters. It got the focus off him." Asked about what it's like to produce a painting during the course of a show in which he'll also move back and forth to sing vocals, play the trumpet, or beat on some drums, he replies that it can be exhilarating or horrifying.

For Connie, even more was at stake than nervousness about the painting she had to produce in ninety minutes. In the documentary film *No One Said It Would Be Easy,* Connie talks about the difficulties and rewards of joining Cloud Cult: "From a performing standpoint, I was nervous about getting up on stage, but from a more spiritual standpoint, I knew that I could really call out to my son and connect with him and feel that this is our celebration of his life. At times it was extremely emotional because you're hearing songs and it's bringing back so much. And at times I'd be painting, and I wouldn't even necessarily be thinking about the audience, I was just thinking about my son and the music, and I'd be weeping while I was painting." Joining the band, she says, was two different things: one, painting in front of people, and two, performing with Craig as a way to bring out their relationship with Kaidin.

During the three years that Craig had been compos-ing three Cloud Cult albums and touring, Connie had lived for a year and a half in a northern Minnesota cabin and then had moved to a housing co-op in Duluth. "I started to piece my life back together," she says, mentioning the work in Duluth she did full-time for an environmental nonprofit on children's environ-mental health issues. "Craig and I started to work together again through Cloud Cult and also started to rebuild our friendship and relationship."

Reflecting on these years, Craig says that he and Connie grieved differently, so they decided to live separately, but they eventually went to grieving counseling together: "Gradually we started to regain our inner strength. Once we were able to stand up as individuals again, it was clear to both of us that there was no one else in the world we wanted to be with, and we fell in love all over again. We visited each other often, and she started painting on stage around the Hippo days of 2005, and we moved back in together shortly after."

When rock bands end, personal issues have usually caused splits among the members. For Cloud Cult, perhaps, opposite forces were in play—despite the disappointments with the Happy Hippo tour, Craig needed to keep the band together as a way to help his and Connie's personal issues work themselves out.

An autobiography is a book written by an author about his or her life. The term literally means "self—life—write," and up until the past few decades, most autobiographies were read for the details they provided about the lives of persons who were usually famous or important, the expectation being that the story comes from the ultimate insider view. When literary critics began turning attention to the *autos,* to the performance of self that writing an autobiography requires, the understanding of what qualifies as an autobiography shifted. Unlike traditional autobiographies that cover events chronologically over a span of years, interesting life stories emerged that reshaped the genre. Writers researched and shaped the biography of a parent, which implicitly (and sometimes explicitly) was an autobiographical act. Numerous people wrote illness narratives, accounts of their struggles with a disease that included fascinating information about bodies, minds, or Western and Eastern medicine. A substantial number of writers created travel narratives as much about the ways that traveling shaped their sense of self and changed them as about the places visited.

Like autobiography scholars, critics in other artistic disciplines have begun emphasizing the performance of self that creative expression demands, and when these performances are stretched out over some years, they can be interpreted as autobiography, the self creating a life. *They Live on the Sun* to *Aurora Borealis* to *Advice from the Happy Hippopotamus* demonstrates an arc of grieving that mirrors Minowa's evolving selfhood; that is, Minowa's art shaped into particular albums and supported by concert tours becomes his way of performing selfhood and his place in the world. His art and evolving sense of self then shapes the meaning of his own life story, which shapes his art, which shapes the life, in an endlessly recursive process.

Observers of Cloud Cult's music might disagree on particulars of Minowa's self-creation (as critics have differences of interpretation about literary autobiographies), but few would dispute the central role of the great album *The Meaning of 8* (2007). Perhaps the emotional grief work that went into the earlier albums had given Minowa the distance he needed from his losses to create astonishing art; perhaps his reuniting with Connie or perhaps simply his searching in philosophy and religion allowed him—a musical virtuoso—to make a groundbreaking album. But *The Meaning of 8* made many top ten lists of the year, and the music critic of the *Denver Post,* Ricardo Baca, ranked it as one of the top twelve albums of the decade, along with records by bands the likes of Modest Mouse and Radiohead.

Advice from the Happy Hippopotamus is the artistic and symbolic expression of a deep psychological sojourn, and the album's tour had helped Minowa get better at reaching the Other Side, the spirit world. "The shows were helping with that a lot," he says, "because every night would be a chance to get to a really deep place. And I wasn't needing to be in such a crazed state of mind to reach that space in the studio." His individual psychological journeying led him, when he began writing the songs that would become *The Meaning of 8,* to a broader philosophical and religious sojourn, to pursuing the mystical path: "I decided this album was going to be one attempt after another to connect to the Other Side and get any information possible about this whole mystery. The key to that veil between here and the afterlife had started years before, but by the time of *The Meaning of 8,* my using music as a tool for connecting to the Other Side was an everyday practice, so it followed that the album would just reflect those ongoing pursuits." Believing that Kaidin was still a presence in his life, refusing to accept either the scientific or Christian explanations of death, Minowa looked to a variety of religious and philosophical traditions to find understanding that matched his own experience and intuition.

In the liner notes of *The Meaning of 8,* Minowa explains that Carl Jung, searching for universal symbols that would show the connected unconscious among all humans, found one such symbol in the number eight. And Minowa goes on to list religions and philosophies that have seen special significance in that number: Indian Jainists with their eight chakras, and Indian Hindus with their eight-armed goddess, Devi, who represents the totality of the universe; Buddhists with their eightfold Path; Cabalists, who argue that the Temple of Jerusalem contained eight gates, the eighth opening only for the Messiah; Muslims, who believe in eight paradises, where the saved will be accompanied by eight animals; ancient Babylonians, who thought the universe was made of eight realms, and in the eighth realm the gods lived with the dead; mathematicians who made the symbol of infinity an eight laid sideways. "Two infinite circles attached side by side,"

Minowa writes, "make the number 8. Thus, the Pythagoreans saw the number 8 as the symbol for infinite love. Similarly, 8 is the first cubic root, representing, for Pythagoreans, the infinity created in the love of the trinity of family—father, mother, and child (2×2×2)." My examples here are only a fraction of what Minowa cites, and you could listen to this album and be intrigued without reading the liner notes, but various songs are enriched by this knowledge. In the song "2×2×2," for example, Minowa sings, "Shape the pain into something great / Disintegrate and reintegrate," because the end result can be love and family.

Minowa's philosophic and religious searching had begun earlier in his life, though without the urgency that followed Kaidin's death. Minowa had an upbringing heavy in Christian literature and Bible study, but he says that his "most weathered book at home is a book about the various world religions. I enjoy trying to find the similarities." He took philosophy in college, which didn't fill the hunger in him, and he turned at one point to studying Native American religious traditions. He "messed with" paganism, read up on Scientology. For about a year he was an Eckankar member, a relatively new religion that combines ideas from a variety of religions and emphasizes personal spiritual experiences as the way to God. Minowa then became influenced greatly by Buddhism. He read the Book of Thomas and noted that the early Christian church kicked out this book because it showed that Jesus, who grew up near an area with a strong Buddhist influence, had some strong Eastern philosophical leanings. "No mass religion," he says, "is a perfect fit for me; yet I would argue that given an open enough mind, a person can find spiritual comfort and guidance in any of them. Ultimately, the path to God is the one less taken. So you kind of have to expect to wander the woods alone in a lot of ways."

A religious mystic is someone who believes in the existence

of realities beyond human comprehension, and the spiritual journey for most mystics is to lose the self in pursuit of communion with these ultimate realities. Minowa's search led him to ways of expressing the collapse of categories such as life and death. The philosophy/religion known as Spiritualism is one such way, having its roots in the writings of Emanuel Swedenborg, who claimed to communicate with angels in heaven and hell and who was influential enough to create a new Christian sect, the Church of New Jerusalem. For Swedenborgians, humans have a physical and spiritual component to their beings, and after death only the physical disappears. In late nineteenth-century America, Spiritualism, with its focus on "mediums" who make contact with the spirit world, had millions of members. Believers flocked to living rooms of these mediums, who told them messages about the afterlife from dearly departed spirits. In "Your 8th Birthday" from *The Meaning of 8,* Minowa communicates with one such person, the song being a tribute to his dead son and what he might be doing in some other realm: "Who could hang a dead man's swing-set from the moon? / Yeah, you did, then you gave it / To the ghosts and the witches." The images evoke the world of an eight-year-old, which Kaidin would have been at this time, a world that is pleasant enough even if a bit macabre. But the song has a chorus, repeated three times, that is simply Minowa wailing "Kaidin" in extended measures. Minowa seems to be calling his son, if not to reappear in body, to be present again in spirit, and a subject that many people would shy away from because its intense emotion becomes uplifting here, even joyful.

During the time of writing the album's songs, Minowa has said, he was summoning spirits by bashing on the sheetrock of his studio. Such moments provided the material for one of the album's great songs, a song characteristic of Cloud Cult's over-the-top reach for the transcendent. In the very slow-paced "Dance for the

Dead," Minowa sings in a shaky voice, accompanied by a softly strumming acoustic guitar: "This is the dance that brings the dead to the living / Just say 'I miss you, every day you know.'" After a shimmery instrumental break, the second verse repeats the words but now from the point of view of the dead, who say, "I'm with you, every day you know." This call and response is repeated, and then the song gets weird and really good. First Minowa and then the rest of the band members begin chanting together very slowly, "Can you hear them come? Can you hear them come?" with the last "come" drawn out over several measures. The drums add a heavy beat, and foot stomping accentuates the sense that tired people are trudging to this place. Amid gorgeous cello and violin lines, the voices then begin to swell in what sounds like six-part harmony, with occasional soaring voice breaks from the melody. The line is repeated eight times, with the singing getting louder and louder, with more instruments added in each time. Finally, Minowa, alone again, comes back to the verse and sings, "I miss you, every day you know." "Dance for the Dead" works as a Spiritualist moment—not quite elegy, certainly not lament—with Cloud Cult serving as their own musical medium.

In a 2011 concert at Orchestra Hall in Minneapolis, the band played "Dance for the Dead" as one of its encores. Minowa introduced it as a song meant to put us in touch with those who have passed, and the band had about thirty people materialize on stage during the song. From my seat near the front, it sounded as if all 2,500 people in the audience were singing "can you hear them come," and the emotion in the theater was electrifying. I saw people with tears in their eyes, and I felt my own. A friend of mine, Eric Nelson, who hadn't been to a rock concert in years but was intrigued by my interest in Cloud Cult, was at this show and wrote me afterward that the audience was an experience in itself: "I've never before been in such a large group of religious fanatics.

We left after two encores, before people started coming to the stage to be washed in the blood of the lamb." Our culture has an unease generally with public displays of intense emotion, as well as displays of "non-normal" thinking, but it's a testament to Cloud Cult that in concert, moments such as this one are simply celebrated communally.

Mystics from all religions are united by the desire to experience unity, the similar essential qualities of all things human and nonhuman, animate and nonanimate. But this mystical experience always eludes rational thought and words, because a person cannot describe but can only testify about or point toward the indescribable. The difficulty for mystics who wish to go beyond their own self-enclosed world comes in how to do that testifying or pointing, how to show others what is luminous and ephemeral. Perhaps *The Meaning of 8*'s starkest experiment of creating the luminous occurs with the song "Everywhere All at One Time." A short instrumental, the song blends together collage-like overlays such as loon calls, Kaidin (or some other child) laughing, stringed instruments, a woman speaking a foreign language, and a man talking, among other noises. Perhaps it's not even a song—one could argue that it's just gobbledygook—but it does convey some of what impinges on the conscious and unconscious minds "all at one time."

In his liner notes, Minowa made clear his belief that in most of the world's great religions the number eight has held special significance as a gateway between the material world we know and the spirit world we intuit or feel. The album's extraordinary artwork, all done by Connie Minowa and Scott West, reinforces the central metaphor of the meaning of eight. The foldable CD case has four panels on each side: three are taken up by liner notes, credits, and song titles, but the other five are paintings that represent various songs. One panel has Kaidin's likeness, with photos, his artwork, and pets circling him. Another features Craig, in a black spandex-like spacesuit with the numeral 8 on it, dancing with a skeleton while crowds watch and a figure bathed in light orchestrates the scene. Another panel depicts a Garden of Eden: Adam and Eve on one side look young and in love; in the middle, two unisex faces overlap with the numeral 8 on each forehead; a dove of peace flies through the landscape; all the figures are enveloped in two ovals that at first look like glasses or eggs but in this context function as the numeral 8 lying sideways.

As beautiful and symbolic as the art is and as interesting as the liner notes are, an album still is a collection of songs that have to work as music. What makes *The Meaning of 8* such an exhilarating listening experience, particularly the deeper one gets into the album, is how Minowa dances his songs around his central concepts, letting the songs exist as separate and interesting pop songs on their own but having them interact in marvelous small ways. In this, the album is like Neutral Milk Hotel's classic *In the Aeroplane over the Sea,* which Jeff Mangum has said was inspired by his reading of Anne Frank's *The Diary of a Young Girl* and his own recurring dreams of a Jewish family during World War II. In songs such as "King of Carrot Flowers" and "Two-Headed Boy," with their wild instrumentation and passionate but obscure lyrics, Mangum gives us not the story of Anne Frank that we all know but a tapestry of emotional art in response to that story. In *The Meaning of 8,* Minowa likewise doesn't preach a mystical philosophy or religion but uses his exploration of mysticism to create shining small jewels of song that reflect his personal seeking.

Only a few of the songs from *The Meaning of 8* address life and death directly; most are concerned with taking a sideways glance at how we might live. A typical song shows the speaker in a stage of becoming, here and now in this world. Minowa emphasizes moments where our usual state of being is either confounded or blurred, a state not negative as our culture would have it, but positive in the way of the mystical seeker. The speaker in "Chemicals Collide," for example, says, "I was out paying close attention, or was I lost inside my thoughts / These days it's hard to tell what's outside from what's in my mind." In the opening song, "Chain Reaction," a drumbeat of African rhythms combines with violins and guitar to quietly set the mood, then Minowa sings alone the line "You have eyes like mine," followed by another singer joining, "Are we strangers or am I you are I." The music swells as both sing the line "Put your face on mine," which works as union (two lives into one) and as overlay that emphasizes similarities. The song then suggests a Buddhist interconnectivity: "Put out fear and they'll feel fear / Put out love and they'll feel love / It's a chain reaction." In one of the final songs on *The Meaning of 8,* "The Deaf Girl's Song," Minowa breaks logical connections. Someone sing us a song, he says, "that makes us feel like raspberries in the middle of June," and the one who does is a deaf girl, whose three-minute song of silence goes number one on the radio and is "the best damn gift for everyone." The deaf girl's song teaches us to see by hearing silence, the end result being the Buddhist-like notion that she'll "make the world stand still." Minowa boldly follows this track later with his own silent song, a blank track that interrupts the listening experience.

The Meaning of 8 uses imagery and ideas of numerous religions without privileging any one. God on this album, for example, may be a divine being, but God is manifested on earth in misconceptions and ordinary matters. In "A Good God," Minowa sees God who turns out to be an eighty-year-old dog, a little girl kissing a frog, and a little boy who thought Jesus was He-Man. Or in the strange story song "Alien Christ," a rocket crash is interpreted as being either a missile, or aliens, or the return of Jesus to earth; long after everyone has lost interest in the story, a girl who was born a few years later and who has never spoken but only laughed, says with her first words at eight years old: "Someone as God came / And ran its fingers through my hair."

In *The Meaning of 8* Minowa's persona is the mystic whose spiritual searching in the face of tragedy has finally reached a resting point, a confidence in the goodness of life. The song "Purpose" argues that there must be a design of some kind on earth. And why? Because life is "so unexpectedly predictable / So sloppily intentional." Perhaps nothing shows Minowa's emotional state of being better than the simple titles of several songs in the second half of this album: "Purpose," "Thanks," and "Hope." In the beautiful acoustic song "Thanks," Minowa says that living is wonderful because everything is so beautiful. "And I give thanks to my present day," he sings: "It just got here so please don't go away / I finally see it's what I choose to make / I choose to make it into gold." Not only are the lyrics optimistic on *The Meaning of 8* when compared to the earlier albums, but the sound is warmer, more orchestral and melodic. Mostly gone are the ambient noises, the computer samples, and the prerecorded drumbeats—the sounds that a composer, sitting in his studio with a computer, is tempted to use. Minowa de-emphasizes the synthesizer on this album, even the electric guitar. Violin and cello together are prominent, and the rhythms of songs are carried not only by bass and drums but by acoustic guitar. There's even some trumpet and trombone.

What most fans think of as the "Cloud Cult sound" probably begins with *The Meaning of 8,* when the band blends guitar-based rock, multiple vocal parts, the occasional ambient sound, and orchestral chamber pop. My favorite description of that evolving sound comes from the music features editor at *Philthy Blog,* Izzy Cihak, who reaches to describe the nearly indescribable: "Aside from being an art rock band in possibly the most literal sense of the phrase of all-time, [Cloud Cult's] sound is some-thing along the lines of postmodern, space age, folky indie pop. It's progressively organic and electronically-anti-pretty-much-everything-associated-with-the-phrase-'electronic.' I would say it's something that needs to be experienced to be understood but, like the work of William S. Burroughs and David Lynch, there's a good chance that even after experiencing it you won't entirely understand it . . . but that doesn't mean that it won't rock your socks."

The music that can rock your socks—or make you want to dance or make love—has often been criticized for its emphasis on the body over the mind, for its emphasis on instinct and feeling rather than the training and rationality of classical music. In his book *The Triumph of Vulgarity: Rock Music in the Mirror of Roman-ticism*, Robert Pattison laments how social refinement and taste have been replaced by the vulgarity and excess that he equates with the emotion created by rock music. Allan Bloom in *The Clos-ing of the American Mind* asserts with great certainty that "rock music has one appeal only, a barbaric appeal, to sexual desire—not love, not *eros*, but sexual desire undeveloped and untutored." In such music there is nothing "noble, sublime, profound, deli-cate, tasteful, or even decent," Bloom says; rock music has "room only for the intense, changing, crude, and immediate." These dia-tribes (and Pattison and Bloom are only two critics among many) do make sense if your desire is primarily to process life ratio-nally more than to feel emotionally, and do make sense if you only know songs such as the Rolling Stones' "Jumping Jack Flash" or Led Zeppelin's "Whole Lotta Love."

Cloud Cult's music counters such antirock assertions, as it appeals to the mind as much as the body, to beauty as much as sex. Some songs sound like the quirky yet beautiful lyrics and sonics of Neutral Milk Hotel with Brian Eno plugging his ambient noises in the music's gaps, all underscored with the over-the-top passion of Arcade Fire. Other songs are nothing like those, more perhaps like the psychedelic-tinged sounds of Animal Collective or Tame Impala. But it's not easy to compare Cloud Cult to other bands. The music appeals, most of all, to the spirit and the soul.

A song that demonstrates the evolved sonic qualities in combination with a lyric full of contradictions and strange moments is the marvelous "Take Your Medicine." As with many of Cloud Cult's complex songs, the emotions of the song can't be comprehended immediately, nor does the verse and chorus structure allow for quick recognition. The song begins with some fuzzed-out guitar noise and a drumbeat, creating an eerie feel accentuated when a bass melody line enters, followed by fast strumming from the electric guitar. Cello and violin help carry the rhythm with indistinct pizzicato, and then Minowa joins in vocally, singing a lyric that will tell a common story of someone beginning over. But this lyric and music are hardly your usual pop song.

Minowa weaves three story threads together in this song and then closes with a twist on one of them. The first thread concerns the speaker not being so hard on himself, as he has been for years. "Remind, remind," he says, "That it's bigger than me," a line that he follows with the enigmatic, koan-like Buddhist saying: "dissolve, dissolve, into evergreens." A beautiful cello, violin, and piano melody comes in at this point, supported by guitar and drums to give the song a driving rhythm, as if something is resolved, only to return after twenty-five seconds back to the fuzzed-out sound, to a small shift in rhythm, and then to a melody played on glockenspiel, accompanied only by Minowa's vocal with all other instruments silent:

> These are things that I keep hidden in my belly.
> I can't see them but they control my life.

> For a moment you could see right through me,
> See right through me, help me make this right.
> Look at all of those skeletons running
> From their closets, get them in the light.

As a description of how we hold bodily our damaging emotions and can only get away from these "skeletons" through understanding and help from others, these images are superb. And when Minowa sings the verse again, and instruments join—first bass, then drums, then guitar, and finally a jazzy synthesizer—it's as if the band or even music itself is getting those skeletons right out there into the light, ready to be dealt with.

Having looked clearly at what runs his life in a bad way, Minowa comes to his third thread, advice that seems hard-won but deservedly so. He introduces the verse with yet another tempo shift and instrument change, as a guitar strums a rhythm for the transition, and then he sings, playing his guitar alone, facing the demons:

> You can take it in stride
> Or you can take it right between the eyes
> Suck up, suck up, and take your medicine
> It's a good day, it's a good day to face the hard things.

If the song hasn't already been complex enough, the final seventy-five seconds are simply a tour de force, a musician and lyricist at the height of his powers weaving the threads together. Musically, Minowa blends elements that dominated previous sections: the glockenspiel solo, a strings melody line, the synthesizer riff, and the guitar. Lyrically, he makes one small change to a verse, suggesting that if you can get rid of the skeletons, you can birth something new: "We found beautiful babies / Sleeping in our ribs / Get them in the light." After singing those lines several times, Minowa shifts to his earlier verse, "You can take it in stride . . . Suck up, suck up, and take your medicine," while other band members sing the "beautiful babies" verse in counterpoint. After repeating these, all instruments fall silent, the two sets of vocals merge, and for one last time, six voices sing, "suck up, suck up, and take your medicine."

The Meaning of 8 debuted at number one on North America's college radio charts in the category of *CMJ* "Most Adds." Its success came not only because of Cloud Cult's popularity with the college crowd, but because the band had become a staple of independent radio stations such as KCMP The Current in the Twin Cities, WNYC in New York, and KEXP in Seattle, which also report to *CMJ*. The album made its way quickly onto the top one hundred of the *CMJ* charts and then onto the top twenty. For the first time the album was appearing in selected record stores, thanks to the band having hired Thaddeus Rudd of The Rebel Group, a small, hard-working firm that does distribution for independent musicians. Even more important, Cloud Cult's new publicist, Sue Marcus at Stunt Company, was deeply immersed in the national music scene and had contacts at *Rolling Stone,* NPR, and other national outlets. Media interest picked up.

Various print publications from newspapers to magazines to blogs were praising the album. *Spin* magazine named Cloud Cult as a breaking band. Hipsters in the blogosphere who usually embrace irony were allowing Cloud Cult a free pass, often exclaiming that the sentimentalism or self-help qualities in the songs were well deserved, given the Minowas' personal story. Cloud Cult was also getting the kind of attention for its environmental principles for which a small band could only dream. MTV came to Sandstone to do a feature. "The place is so far out in the boonies, you can barely find it, because it's not on the maps," said Dan Montalto, the producer who brought a camera crew to the farm to film a short feature on the band. On camera, Minowa articulately discussed the band's environmental principles and music, and the interview along with footage of the farm and the recording studio was posted on May 11, 2007. On NPR's *Morning Edition* for June 21, host Steve Inskeep reported on the environmental hazards in the music industry, lamenting that MP3 players contain heavy metals and chemicals and many CDs come in plastic jewel cases. After noting that some labels had begun sending advance copies of albums only digitally, and other labels had quit using plastic cases in favor of recyclable paperboard CD cases, he concluded by saying, "our eco-award goes to the tiny label Earthology Records, which is based on a geothermal and wind-powered farm. The company prints its recycled CD cases with soy ink."

Cloud Cult made its debut for its new national tour by playing a showcase at SXSW in Austin in March. The band had a new bass player, Matthew Freed, who had production experience and who corecorded, coengineered, and coproduced *The Meaning of 8* with Minowa. By happenstance, Jeff Johnson came on board, who has gone on to play a vital role for Cloud Cult as its sound technician and tour manager. Johnson had worked two Cloud Cult shows when he was sound technician at the Varsity Theater in Minneapolis, and he was impressed by their level of gratitude and humility compared to most of the acts he helped. Johnson wanted to get down to SXSW without buying an airline ticket; seeing that Cloud Cult was doing a showcase, he offered to run sound for free if he could hitch a ride. The entire experience went well, and Johnson joined the tour, opening for Cloud Cult as an acoustic singer–songwriter and running the soundboard for the show. Though he hasn't always continued to play his own music, Johnson has accompanied Cloud Cult on all its subsequent tours. "I'm not part of this entourage because I want to be a sound manager for a rock band," he says. "I'm getting to be part of a band that asks all the right spiritual questions."

After playing SXSW and then performing a CD release party in Minneapolis on March 30, Cloud Cult hit the road. With this tour Cloud Cult became known as a great live band, a reputation that helped grow the fan base. Reviews of the live show, including strong praise from Nate Chinen of the *New York Times* after a concert at the Mercury Lounge, generated interest. Connie Minowa and Scott West had become band members, which was always mentioned in the advance publicity; while most people view paintings in their final state, either in an exhibit or museum, Cloud Cult concertgoers were enjoying art in process, watching two paintings emerge, which would be auctioned off for charity at the end of the show. The visual also extended to the band on stage. Needing to enlarge the band's sound to play the new songs, Minowa hired a violinist, Shannon Frid (now Frid-Rubin), to join them on tour. Frid and Sarah Young provided a strong string presence and, along with Connie, a strong visual balance to the men. Most of the new album's songs were written for the band, and with minimal computer additions they could be played easily in the shows. "Pretty Voice," "Chemicals Collide," "Please Remain Calm," and "Take Your Medicine," among numerous others, became concert standards. The band's concert success was also coming from its own understanding of how to structure musically a concert's emotional arc.

In her poem "The Summer Day," the best-selling American poet Mary Oliver begins by asking who made the world and who made the black bear and the grasshopper that has landed on her hand and that she's looking at closely enough that she can see its jaws and eyes and forearms. Saying that she doesn't know exactly what prayer is, Oliver notes that she does know how to pay attention, how to be idle and blessed. It's this sense of prayer as rapt attention that Cloud Cult wants its music to demonstrate, an attention that opens up the entire world to you and your heart. In concert, Cloud Cult asks its audience implicitly to enter into the ceremony that is its stage show and therefore to think about what it means to be entertained. The concert stage is sacred territory, says Minowa, and beginning with this tour the band opened concerts with "Hope," a quiet song that builds slowly and has only three lines, all of which are sung numerous times. Juxtaposing the phrase *holding hope* next to *holding still,* the song, Minowa has said, "set a sense of prayer"; rather than opening with an up-tempo song to get everyone jumping around and pumped up, Cloud Cult invited the audience into "the ritual that is a live performance."

Those live performances were exhausting, as the band played nearly every night, taking a day off only when they were driving hundreds of miles. But although venues were still small and sometimes not full, the tour was producing word-of-mouth excitement. After crisscrossing the country in April and May, Cloud Cult returned home to Minnesota, playing shows in Duluth and in Minneapolis at First Ave. While the conventional wisdom had always been that a band could oversaturate a market—that the number of fans was finite, and people would space out their times seeing any one band—Cloud Cult found its audiences in the Twin Cities getting bigger and more enthusiastic the more it played. Andrea Swensson, who began the websites Reveille Magazine and Gimme Noise and presently works for KCMP The Current in the Twin Cities, believes that an interest in local music was then picking up steam the way interest had been growing with the local artisans and the local foods movements. The globalization of music, she says, means that someone in Minneapolis can be listening to music made from anywhere on earth—with YouTube and streaming radio stations and downloads off Internet sites, music from anywhere is readily available. "While on one hand this is great," she continues, "the Internet and computers can make you feel really isolated. Getting into a local band means the fan can have a different relationship with the band, one where they hear the band play live regularly, where they might meet them and talk to them." Cloud Cult band members always appear after a concert to talk to fans and to sit at the merchandise table. And people who did meet the band personally sang their praises, in print or to their friends.

With band buzz getting louder, the weekly newspaper *Twin Cities Metro* decided to do a story on Cloud Cult in connection with the show at First Ave on June 29. The web editor for the newspaper, John Paul Burgess, a recent college graduate and would-be filmmaker, thought the paper should have some concert footage to link to the article. With Cloud Cult's permission he filmed the concert using three cameras, one on each wing and one in the back, what he now calls "a real guerrilla operation." After *Twin Cities Metro* had posted footage of several songs on its website, Adrian Young, Cloud Cult's manager, called Burgess, told him that the band really liked his footage, and asked if he would go out on tour with them for a few weeks to make a concert DVD. With Burgess the band headed north to Toronto and Montreal and down the East Coast, playing Boston again and New York, though this time at a bigger venue, the Bowery Ballroom. They went to Philadelphia and then headed west through the heartland: Columbus, Cincinnati, and on to Kansas and Colorado again. For these concerts Burgess took footage of the band himself with a handheld camera, but for the tour's concluding concert on November 15 at Minneapolis's Varsity Theater, he was able to use eight cameras and more sophisticated recording equipment. Some of this concert footage from *The Meaning of 8* tour would become part of a feature-length film released in 2009, *No One Said It Would Be Easy.*

The increase in media attention and in the number of fans coming to concerts helped Minowa enlarge his e-mail database and his hits on the Cloud Cult website. Using his programming skills, Minowa had made the website personal and interactive, good for acquiring e-mail addresses and keeping fans informed. Although his web store didn't have a huge amount of traffic, he had figured out a way to keep most of the money spent there by doing all the mailing himself, a practice that began initially because no mailing service would take the environmental measures that the Minowas wanted. "My biggest blessing at the time, in regards to the web store," he recalls, "was that it was really personalized. When people ordered stuff, it came out of our house. So if they needed something really unique, we could provide that. If there was some kind of error and a customer was upset, we could work directly with that person and make sure they were taken care of. Usually, they'd be so happy that they were actually working with the band, instead of some order bank, that they'd e-mail a nice story about what the band means to them, and we could e-mail back, and sometimes create a whole friendship out of the exchange."

A business strategy that puts environmental practices as a top priority, a strategy that emphasizes direct service and creates friendships—these are not the usual ways to grow, but they were working for Cloud Cult. The band still wasn't making money on the road, but it was close to breaking even. Minowa compares its slow, gradual growth to organic gardening: "When you grow things organically, it takes a lot of time. You've got to build topsoil and balance the nutrients naturally. The plants grow slow and steady, but the roots are deep. In contrast, a lot of bands who explode into the limelight are like conventional gardening. You put a shot of fertilizer on a plant, and its growth explodes, but its root base is pretty shallow."

Touring is necessary as it helps get a band's name out there with the media and puts the band in front of fans; in Cloud Cult's case, the long van rides, which often prove tiresome and irritating, were inadvertently proving also to be a different kind of fertile ground. It's a Cloud Cult tradition that whoever drives the van chooses what music to play. Minowa always chooses to have it quiet, because, as he says, "there's something about driving that lets me hear things in myself very clearly. Some of my best stuff has come out on long road trips. If you sit in the quiet long enough, there comes a point where the music playing on the inside is practically as loud as what you'd hear if you actually put the radio on." Many new songs were coming to him on these van trips or at other moments during this tour. Minowa recalls driving along some country roads in the South, with most of the band asleep, and starting to hear a song and words. "By the time my driving shift was over," he recalls, "I remember just laying down in the back of the van with my notebook and charting out what I heard, including the lyrics. It was pretty much done, front to back, because it was playing so loud inside, I couldn't question anything about it." As soon as the tour was over, that song, "When Water Comes to Life," and others were getting laid down in his basement studio.

Fans Write

I'd just started falling in love when I fell in love with Cloud Cult's music. Three years later, both loves are stronger than ever, and they're inseparable because the band offers a perfect soundtrack for life through simple binaries: grandiosity and intimacy, passion and calm, beauty and imperfection, understanding and unknowing. The music seems crafted to grow with its listeners, through thick and thin, and I couldn't be happier that it's growing with the two of us.

—Luke Ramsay, 21, Allentown, Pennsylvania

The first time I ever heard Cloud Cult, I was on a walk by myself in Seattle, and it was rainy as usual. I was fifteen at the time, and I had downloaded a KEXP Music That Matters podcast and was listening to it as I walked to get coffee or a snack—I don't quite remember. Then, the song "Your Eighth Birthday" came on the podcast, and within forty seconds of the song, I stopped walking and just listened. I had never heard anything like it before. I think I stood, just listening, at this corner by a gas station for the rest of the song and then listened to it again and again for the entirety of the walk (which required scrolling back to the exact second that the song started in the podcast). I had always really enjoyed music, but this was the first time I ever felt so connected to a lyric in such a deep, indescribable way.

It was also the first time that my favorite band remained my favorite band for more than a few months. When I was seventeen, I worked at a camp, and one of my fellow counselors also loved Cloud Cult, and we talked about this indescribable connection that we both have to Cloud Cult. At the end of the summer she gave me a small notebook full of lines from songs. I took this book to college, and both the notebook and the music helped me immensely (especially the song "Everybody Here Is a Cloud") when my friend from high school died three weeks into my first year of college.

It has been five years since I first heard "Your Eighth Birthday" on that street corner, and in those five years I haven't stopped listening to Cloud Cult, and they haven't stopped being my favorite band.

—Rachael Haensly, 20, Seattle, Washington

When I listen to Cloud Cult, I remember to forget my fear and instead feel connected, sometimes in a giddy sense, sometimes in a sad but compassionate sense. Life is hard but what a freakin' trip!

—A. Bloodgood, 46, Austin, Texas

I distinctly remember the first time I heard Cloud Cult. I was sitting in the loft room of a communal barn during one of my yearly trips to southern Oregon. I was surrounded by my dear family and ever-growing community of clowns, freaks, faeries, and shamans. I was midsentence in a conversation about community manifestation and spiritual motivation when I heard the lyric "someone turn the lights out, there's so much more to see in our darkest places." I immediately went downstairs, thinking maybe someone

had grabbed a guitar and was just singing their heart out. I was half right; the amazing symphony of instruments and lyrical magic that were pouring from the CD player was in fact coming directly from the heart, and it was connected to my heart. Thus began my eternal dance with Cloud Cult. I dove into their discography, each song a new discovery of awareness and beauty.

I remember being so immediately enamored that I reached out to Craig directly just to introduce myself and share my enthusiasm for the gift he was giving the world. I meekly asked for a section of sheet music for a song I wanted to get inked on my arm. Craig lit up at the idea of me having their music tatted, apologized for not having sheet music for that particular piece, but gave me the major chords and wished me luck on figuring it out. And I did.

I flew to Portland to witness Cloud Cult live, an experience I hope everyone gets to have at least once. At the Portland show I approached the band with the piece of sheet music I had compiled from listening to my favorite song, "Journey of the Featherless." This was the sheet music that would later be tattooed on my arm in tribute, along with the lyric "my heart's still beating, guess i'm pretty lucky." I have numerous tattoos but can say without a doubt that my sleeve of music is my most precious, the most emotional, and the most real. I had them all sign that little piece of sheet music, a piece of paper I now have framed on my wall.

I cannot fully express how Cloud Cult makes me feel, how the sound of Craig's voice with the mix of Arlen's beats and Shannon's violin brings a smile to my face and warms my soul. I can only show my appreciation for them as a band and as human beings by sharing their music with every single person I encounter.

—Chandra Krinsky, 27, Berkeley, California

Truthfully, I think of Cloud Cult as my religion. When I'm questioning my purpose, luck, relationships, future, or my impending doom, Cloud Cult reminds me that I'm human, and that I'm OK. Listening to their music is kind of like taking in a deep breath of air after crying. It restores me with life, and I'm able to laugh at the things that get me down. That's more than a therapist has done for me in three years.

Below the surface, knowing Cloud Cult's history with the loss of their beautiful son, Kaidin, reminds me that the band is something like a breathing human being who has felt loss and deep sadness and that produces emotions and actions as a result. With the band's humanization has come a deeper connection for everyone who has heard their story. I haven't experienced loss yet, and I'm so scared to, but I feel like Cloud Cult will be the first to console me. Their music fits every moment in my life, and I feel as if their sound and meaning have reached deep within me, intertwining and building everything that I believe in: fresh starts, love, escaping, strength, simplicity, beauty, and the unknown. I can and I will face everything with Cloud Cult by my side.

—Riga Cavanaugh, 15, St. Paul, Minnesota

When I first listened to Cloud Cult, it felt like I just had my heart ripped out and they happened to be following me around in case I needed a donor. Every song is a story that brings to light buried emotions, some of which I had never experienced before. *Feel Good Ghosts* is one of my favorite albums; its beautiful sonic creativity and grounding lyrics guide me to focus on love, relationships, and becoming a more purposeful human being with the time that has been given to me. "Everybody here is a cloud. Everybody here will evaporate. You came up from the ground, from a million little pieces. Have you found where your place is?"

—Wayne Hacker, 28, Muskegon, Michigan

was enraptured as always and blessed to be in the company of people I loved. I cannot say what the song was, but there she was, perhaps ten feet from me, wracked with sobs, twisting a thin scarf in her hands. I moved to her and put my arms around her, held her, rocked her, loved her through whatever the song was that owned her heart, and I prayed the tears helped, and the embrace helped, and the song helped whatever it was that hurt so. I said something, perhaps "darling, let them heal you, they are so powerful."

"It's so big, you have no idea," she replied. She told me she was from Canada, and she had driven all the way alone to see Cloud Cult, and it was the first time. I told her to go to the merchandise tent, as they often appeared after their concerts. And we drifted away into our lives.

A few months later, we watched from the front row as Cloud Cult performed at Orchestra Hall. After the concert, a couple approached me and said they recognized me from the Duluth concert and where was my friend tonight and how was she? I explained I did not know her or her story but surmised it was a terrible thing. They told me they had met her at the merchandise tent, and she was grieving the loss of her child.

I sometimes regret I have no way to go back and extend that moment with her, to take her to dinner that night, and send her on her way back to Canada as my friend. But mostly I think what we shared was exactly as it was meant to be. Such connections and stories happen over and over surrounding Cloud Cult, who remind us we are all too human, sometimes things are really awful, and we can be good to ourselves and each other. That is a noble message, and we are listening.

—Denise Beck, 55, Minneapolis, Minnesota

The first time I heard *The Meaning of 8* I was in a car with four coworkers from the New York State Museum in Long Island. We were heading out to dinner, and one of them, Chris, put in the CD that he had purchased the previous weekend. Who knew that moment would be a pivotal moment in my life.

Around the same time I was rediscovering my spirituality and faith. Cloud Cult has become the soundtrack to that journey in several ways. One is that Craig Minowa's lyrics got me rethinking my own faith in ways I had not explored since I was an inquisitive youth in Sunday school. Two is the live shows transported me to a place that I had only experienced worshipping in an Orthodox church during my time in Cyprus. It was the closest I felt to God in a long time, and it rekindled in me what had been dormant. The music, the painting, the whole experience of Cloud Cult performing live is really otherworldly and transports you away from the Bowery Ballroom, First Avenue, wherever they happen to be performing that night, to somewhere else entirely. The fact they were from Minnesota got me thinking that if something as cool as Cloud Cult came out of Minnesota, it might not be a bad place to relocate.

As my faith and spirituality grew, I began to get the call to ordained ministry and in fact have moved to Minnesota, where I am now a student at Luther Seminary and serving a yearlong internship in Rochester, Minnesota. And I can honestly say I would not be where I am, the happiest and fullest I've ever felt, without Cloud Cult. Craig's lyrics can articulate things that at times I cannot, and I have used the songs as sermon illustrations, confirmation tools, and really wherever I can get the opportunity to share the Gospel of Cloud Cult.

—David Hanssen, 29, Rochester, Minnesota

the Message Established
LOVE AND LIGHT

On April 8, 2008, Cloud Cult released its album *Feel Good Ghosts (Tea-Partying through Tornadoes)*. The album's songs have little of the angst and confusion of *They Live on the Sun* or *Aurora Borealis,* and little of the philosophical and psychological searching that we see in *Advice from the Happy Hippopotamus* or *The Meaning of 8.* In an interview with *Rolling Stone,* Minowa said the album "brings closure to a lot of the storylines involved in the grieving process, and moves into a rebirth process." As suggested in the album's title, the ghosts here are comforting, not scary. They aren't the skeletons in closets whom Minowa wants to get into the light in "Take Your Medicine." These new songs are confident in their personal and environmental messages.

Sarah Young, the band's former cellist, says of Minowa that he is very passionate about his ideals, which are environmentalism and love. This album and the subsequent tour consolidated the message and sound that he had been working toward for several years. In the album's final song, "Love You All," the band plays the same simple melody line numerous times, set in counterpoint against a verse that works as a chorus: "I love my mother, I love my father / And when it's my time to go, I need you to know / I love you all." The verse is sung six times; the first two by Minowa, then with descant, twice more in harmony, and finally solo by Minowa without instrumentation. No song could be an easier critical target for a cynic or a hipster, in part because no song lays out this message in such a near-naive, heartfelt way. But a measure of what Cloud Cult had come to mean for its fans by 2008 was that night after night on the tour, hundreds of people, many with tears, sang the verse along with the band.

The songs on *Feel Good Ghosts* have the usual Cloud Cult experimentations: live drums mixed with computerized drumbeats, arrangements that feature driving bass lines and up-tempo electric guitar riffs alongside orchestral pop, lyrics that span the range of the very witty to the nearly inane, which Minowa somehow pulls off with humor. The album acknowledges a personal history, but the songs mostly reference that history for those already in the know. The first song is the bouncy "No One Said It Would Be Easy," which opens with an engaging arpeggio riff of piano and synthesizer, followed by the entire band singing "how long" seven times. Explanations and resolutions on this album's songs often come through a merge of science and art, as in the following stanza about birth: "You were sewn together with a tapestry of molecules / A billion baby galaxies and wide open spaces." Minowa follows this scientific metaphor with lines that continue the wordplay: "And everything you need is here, everything you fear is here / And it's holding you up, it just keeps holding you up." The song works for any listener, in the sense that the "it" can be any difficulty that someone has, or the "it" can be something like faith that keeps one afloat. The song, of course, means something more for Cloud Cult fans, who may interpret the following lines in light of the Minowas' story of loss, grief, and recovery: "When it all comes crashing down / Try to understand your meanings / No one said it would be easy."

The intertwining of the scientific and personal continues with the album's second song, the concert favorite "Everybody

Here Is a Cloud," which suggests that we all come from the ground and from a million little pieces, and that we all should try to find our place in the world before we finally evaporate and become like clouds. The music is complex in its rhythms and arrangement, and finally transcendent in its descant and multiple-part harmonies. Minowa sings from a position where personal crisis is behind him and he can dispense advice. "Have you found where your place is?" the song asks repeatedly, and the lyric gives a suggestion for how to do so. Turn the lights out, Minowa sings, because "There's so much more to see in the darkest places."

The powerful song "When Water Comes to Life" about a child autopsy defies expectations in its environmental slant. Unlike the typical songs played at children's funerals, such as Sarah McLachlan's "In the Arms of an Angel" or "God's Will" by Martina McBride, "When Water Comes to Life" doesn't tap into our customary structures and plots in which an innocent child passes far too soon and is taken to heaven by an angel as part of God's will. The song meditates on whether there's a soul, how contradictory human emotions fuel creation of various stories, whether or not an untimely death can lead to healing stories, and yet all such contemplation is balanced by the stark acknowledgment that life into death is also nutrient recycling.

What feels so accepted on this album, and therefore almost nonchalant, is the comfortable presence of otherworldly beings. After Americans' surge of interest in UFO sightings and aliens, the philosopher and secular humanist Paul Kurtz founded in 1976 an organization to investigate paranormal claims from a scientific point of view. The group, now called the Committee for Skeptical Inquiry, has concluded that no paranormal sighting has ever met the standards of scientific scrutiny. But peoples back in time and around the world now have believed in ghosts, and one in four

Americans, despite what the Skeptical Inquirists assert, said in an Associated Press poll in 2007 that they had seen a ghost or felt themselves in the presence of one. Minowa, of course, is among them, believing as he does that Kaidin is not gone, that he lives as energy, as a soul, as a ghost. "We'll start a little family and call it our religion / Hunt for ghosts inside our house cuz we'll never give up wishing / That we live on," he writes in the delightful strings and acoustic guitar piece, "The Ghost inside Our House."

Feel Good Ghosts is deeply serious as in "No One Said It Would Be Easy" or "When Water Comes to Life," but the album is also playful in narrative songs such as "Story of the Grandson of Jesus" or the concert favorite "Journey of the Featherless," where the speaker says that he's ready to leave the earth for a short holiday—or forever. The speaker will decide based on how things go. The long story begins like this:

> I got myself a mission: I'm going to find heaven.
> I made crepe paper wings (I think they'll carry me well).
> I left you a love poem, the best I have written,
> My favorite words were the ones I couldn't spell.
> They say that I'm a lunatic. They say that I am full of it.
> I say that it's worth dreaming, just for the dream of it.
> It's all about passion, it's all about perception.
> Don't call me on my cell phone, cuz there ain't no
>   reception
> When I'm gone.

Off he sets, making friends with the clouds and with the birds: "If you ask a goose a question / He never shuts up." With a rhythm section of strings and catchy percussion, with cello and violin lines weaving in and out of the guitar and bass lines, the song has a vibrant sound to go with its upbeat lyrics.

To promote the album, Cloud Cult made a video for "Everybody Here Is a Cloud," which premiered on the website of *Rolling Stone* in April. The decision to have John Paul Burgess and Scott West create a video came during their making of the documentary *No One Said It Would Be Easy*. Before any real traction was made on the film, the band decided to put the documentary on pause and do a video to coincide with the release of *Feel Good Ghosts*. After hearing a rough cut of "Everybody Here Is a Cloud," Burgess came up with the theme: "I tried to visually depict exactly what the song is about—a literal cloud of people making up all that is, sharing and exchanging molecules in the air between them." He put his ideas on storyboards, presented them to Minowa, West, and Adrian Young, and got the go-ahead.

Since the video shoot needed to be a low-budget affair, the band put out via its e-mail database and Myspace site a call for fans to show up at Como Park in St. Paul on Sunday, March 2. Fans weren't asked to RSVP, and because Burgess really didn't know how many people would come, he created different shot list plans based on the numbers. The day turned up snowy and sleeting. Burgess, West, and three helpful friends arrived early at Como Park, unsure about what was to come. The band arrived, and then about seventy to eighty fans, and the shooting began. No casting, no payments to the extras. "Just a bunch of people in Minnesota," Burgess says, "who decided to show up and jump around in the snow with members of a band that they liked." He admits, having transitioned now into a professional video production career, that the lack of planning was pretty insane: "I can't imagine beginning a shoot with the same naive 'everything will just work out' approach that I did then." But the approach and the resultant video are a genuine and artful example of Cloud Cult's seat-of-the-pants, do-it-yourself ethos.

One striking face in the video is the band's bass player,

Shawn Neary, who had joined Cloud Cult the previous fall, replacing Matthew Freed. Unlike previous Cloud Cult bassists, who stayed in the background, Neary brings his charisma to the forefront in concert, not only playing well off Minowa and conveying great energy, but adding interesting visuals. Neary plays trombone, too, moving back and forth within some songs from brass to bass. Also new to the group was twenty-year-old drummer Arlen Peiffer, replacing Dan Greenwood. Peiffer grew up just outside of Iowa City, Iowa, where as a high-school student he'd go see the punk rock bands at Gabe's Oasis and dream of someday being in a band. A guitarist until his sophomore year, he got a drum set so that friends who wanted to form a band would have a drummer; when he moved to Minneapolis following high school, he got a gig with a local standout singer, Caroline Smith, and then became part of her three-piece backing band, the Good Night Sleeps. But joining Cloud Cult meant getting vaulted onto a national stage—at twenty he was already realizing his dream.

At times the country at large can pinpoint when a band "makes it"; the band gets a single on the radio that goes top ten, for example, or they're invited to play on *Saturday Night Live*. At the music industry level, headlining a showcase at the SXSW Festival in Austin, Texas, is one kind of marker, and that is what Cloud Cult did to critical acclaim a week after making that video in a snowstorm in St. Paul. Andrea Swensson was one of several Minnesotans who got to organize a Minnesota Showcase day at SXSW. On March 15, at the Molotov Lounge, Cloud Cult headlined a party, which also included Doomtree, Kid Dakota, Romantica, and the Alarmists. "Our party was held a little off the beaten path in Austin," Swensson recalls, "and I remember we were nervous that people wouldn't walk that far to come see our bands. But about twenty minutes before Cloud Cult was scheduled to play, the entire place filled up, and we had a packed room for their grand finale." Included in that audience was late-night television host Carson Daly. National blog traffic about Cloud Cult picked up after SXSW, and then again after the release of the album, and even more when *Rolling Stone* named them in its April 16 issue as a Breaking Artist.

Over the next few months, the stars seemed to align for the band, aided, no doubt, by the efforts of its publicist, Sue Marcus. On April 24, Cloud Cult appeared on John Schaefer's influential WNYC's show *Soundcheck,* where the new songs and the band's backstory were heard by the largest public radio audience in the country. WNYC is part of NPR radio, and this appearance marked the beginning of Cloud Cult becoming an NPR darling for its music as well as its environmentalism. On May 10, the *Wall Street Journal* ran a piece, "Taking Art-Rock, Literally," that focused on the painters auctioning their paintings after the show but also described the band's history and principles in an engaging, informative way. For its biggest audience Cloud Cult made its television debut on *Last Call with Carson Daly* on June 17, where about a million viewers watched them play "Story of the Grandson of Jesus." Marcus had first pitched Cloud Cult to Daly's booker a year earlier, in May 2007. She then followed up a few weeks later by sending the MTV film piece and checked in again with Daly's show a week later. She got nowhere with that go-round, but ten months later she pitched the band again twice before the release of *Feel Good Ghosts.* When Daly attended the SXSW set and really liked the band, things moved forward quickly; in late April, the June date was set. The success seemed equal parts a publicist's determination, a band's talent, and serendipity in Daly being taken by a friend to the Cloud Cult SXSW performance.

In June more publicity came the band's way when Cloud Cult got an unlikely shout-out from Josh Radnor, the independent filmmaker and star of the long-running CBS sitcom *How I*

Met Your Mother. Radnor said that although he grew up in Ohio, he had fallen in love with an indie band from Minnesota: "I get a regular newsletter from KEXP, a radio station in Seattle, and they sent out a link to the band's website. I heard the music and went, 'Whoa, this band is amazing!' Their live shows are also fantastic." Radnor included two songs from *The Meaning of 8* in the film he was making at the time, *happythankyoumoreplease,* which won the Audience Award and was nominated for the Grand Jury Prize at the Sundance Film Festival in 2010. Radnor would continue to praise Cloud Cult in public. During his guest deejay stint a year later at KCRW, NPR's flagship station for Southern California and Los Angeles, he compared them to indie royalty: "When I listen to Arcade Fire I feel like the world is ending, and Cloud Cult makes me feel like the world's already ended. . . . Everything's in shards and pieces on the ground, and they're building something new. It's really like this transformative experience listening to them. Their albums are a little bit like operas—it's not like every track is like a single, some of it's just weird and experimental. When people are looking for a new, interesting band that not a lot of people know, I always say Cloud Cult."

The growing national approval of green business and the interest in sustainability fed into Cloud Cult's success, as newspapers, magazines, and blogs all noted the band's environmental principles and commented on Cloud Cult's pioneering environmental role in the music industry. For this tour, Cloud Cult partnered with the green insurance company Esurance, who as a tour sponsor picked up the tab for carbon offsets, subsidized the biodiesel fuel for the van, and printed green tour posters. Esurance also asked Cloud Cult to license a song to use in an advertisement, which Minowa rather surprisingly agreed to. In an interview with Charlie Moran in *Advertising Age,* Minowa explained his thinking: "We've been approached by a number of different companies over the years to use our music for various types of commercials. Because of the extreme environmental ethics of Cloud Cult, we've had to turn down a lot of offers that could have been quite lucrative. . . . I didn't know Esurance very well when they first offered the idea, but I researched the company, and for the first time, I actually felt comfortable doing something like this. We didn't want the commercial to just push insurance or just push our band. We wanted a green message. The whole thing is focused on this sort of fun and artsy way of greening the world, and it ends with a link to a page that offers all sorts of tips on how to make your lifestyle more sustainable." In October Esurance released an animated commercial showing the band members floating on clouds, performing the song "Lucky Today." A short version of the commercial even played the following February during the Super Bowl.

Though Cloud Cult had worked hard at enlarging its e-mail database and had made a website where it could announce concert dates, give the band's history, and sell merchandise, Minowa had not always been savvy about exploiting the new social media that were changing the music business. In particular, the band hadn't been making videos for its earlier albums, though some radio stations' in-studio sessions were on YouTube and on the band's website. With *Feel Good Ghosts* the band began trying harder, including sending out a post to its e-mail database asking for fan-submitted videos. Under the moniker Munkabum, Jon Thompson created an artistic animated video for "When Water Comes to Life." Thompson, now a director at Bolster Agency in Minneapolis, had been a fan of Cloud Cult for years. *Aurora Borealis* was the album that sucked him in, though the live shows also did their part. "One of the most memorable concert experiences," he recalls, "was seeing them at Lakeview Castle in Duluth following a rather hokey all-day UFO convention in the same space.

Cheesy pie-tin UFOs were hanging everywhere, and I remember seeing Mr. Nice, the puppet that was running for mayor in Duluth, dancing in the crowd along with Sasquatches and aliens. Seeing an eclectic Minnesota band with a penchant for the unexplained and the offbeat in this setting was really a dream come true."

Not simply the offbeat attracted Thompson. He says that "When Water Comes to Life" is a comforting and beautiful song for him as a secular humanist with a religious upbringing: "Craig has a wonderful way of merging science and civility with a more mystical realm." Band members liked the video enough that they not only gave Thompson the go-ahead to post it on YouTube, where it has received over 320,000 views, but they asked him to do a second. Like others before him who helped Cloud Cult, Thompson was motivated by the band's music and principles: "They offered me a small amount of money for them [the videos], but I refused because I didn't want it to turn into a business transaction. I was happy to give back to such a family-friendly, noncorporate band that I've benefited so much from."

On the *Feel Good Ghosts* tour, Cloud Cult began an important relationship with another fan, a relationship still continuing. Cody York, a prominent photographer of BMX racing who works for numerous big-name clients, including ESPN and Red Bull, discovered the band's music shortly after caring for his grandfather who had cancer. Feeling scarred by the death of the person who raised him, questioning the purpose of life, York used Cloud Cult's music as a way to think through his own emotions and fears. When he saw that the band was coming to Pittsburgh in November but that two different venues had been announced, he e-mailed the contact on the band's website to ask where the concert would be. He heard back immediately from Minowa himself. Surprised, York then asked if he could shoot some photos during the show and sent a link to his professional website. Minowa said yes, and that the band actually needed a new group portrait: could he do that for them? York has been shooting photos, touring with the band, and making videos with them ever since.

A major label not only does promotion but schedules events such as photo and video shoots for its bands, activities that Cloud Cult has had to arrange for itself and to pay out of pocket, which is why serendipitous encounters with fans such as Thompson and York have sometimes grown into professional arrangements and larger projects. One such project occurred in 2007 with John Paul Burgess, who had been invited to take some footage of the band during *The Meaning of 8* tour, footage that Cloud Cult planned on making into a concert DVD. Those "few weeks on tour" for Burgess would turn into eighteen months when he came to believe that the project should be something different. The band gave him posters and photographs and old video from previous tours; they consented to do interviews; Burgess visited the Minowas' farm in northern Minnesota, recording Craig playing "Transistor Radio" solo on acoustic guitar. And at one point, with all this new and old material, Burgess began putting up storyboards on his apartment walls, imagining how he would tell the band's many stories, how he could avoid strict chronology, how he could not skirt Kaidin's death but how he could avoid making that death the defining event. The concert DVD, in Burgess's mind's eye, had turned into a career-spanning Cloud Cult documentary. Using as a title a recent Cloud Cult song, Burgess, along with Scott West, who did the art for the film, brought *No One Said It Would Be Easy* into being, a title apt for the band's story as well as the film's making.

As he worked on the film, Burgess was surprised at how much freedom he had. West knew how the film was evolving, because he was contributing artwork for many of the scenes, but neither Minowa nor other band members asked Burgess for his vision of the project or critiqued the project in any way. Minowa never even asked to see rough cuts. "The first time that anyone in the band actually saw the film," Burgess recalls, "was in my small apartment, where they all crowded in and watched it on my computer."

On March 22, 2009, *No One Said It Would Be Easy* was screened before a sold-out crowd at the Varsity Theater in Minneapolis. Burgess, West, and Adrian Young made brief comments introducing the film. Most members of the band came, though not the Minowas, Craig writing Burgess that it was the filmmaker's night and he didn't want to take any of the spotlight. The film was a success. David de Young from "How Was The Show?"—an Internet site that reviews the arts in the Twin Cities—talked to prominent members of the local music scene. Barb Abney, a deejay from The Current, commented, "I wasn't prepared for how much I was going to cry. That was amazing. I thought for some reason that it was going to be mostly a live concert DVD, and showing the whole story, there were a lot of things about the band that I didn't know about." Will Michel, from the Bill Mike Band, had a similar reaction: "What exuded in the film was what happened for me seeing them live. There is this universal force of upliftment and musical greatness, really, where each individual person is on their own music journey and excelling at their own craft when they come together. I'm very inspired at this moment. . . . The film is wonderful and captures what's missing from a lot of the music industry, positive messages and musical depth."

A week after the premiere of the film, Cloud Cult hit the road again and played twenty-eight dates in two months, some of them headlining with Margot and the Nuclear So and So's. In April, Cloud Cult played the most prestigious music festival in the United States, Coachella, recognition of the band's growing stature. At the Coachella set, Craig announced that Connie was pregnant and due in the fall, and that the band would take a break. Talking to Ross Raihala from St. Paul's newspaper the *Pioneer Press,* Minowa said that *Feel Good Ghosts* might be the final album: "I don't think there's going to be another Cloud Cult album for a while. It could be never, I don't know." As a last stop, the band played the Cabooze in Minneapolis on August 23, 2009, and called it quits. It was time for the Minowas to shift their attention away from Cloud Cult and toward the new family that was coming into being and toward a new place to call home.

Touring for band members can be exhilarating if the fans show up and are enthusiastic about the music, but touring is also exhausting, which can be exacerbated if the band has little money and is worried about whether it can continue. On this, its fourth national tour, Cloud Cult finally made money after paying overhead and band salaries. The monetary goals were modest, but as Minowa says, "My goal was to get to the point that I actually had money in savings for the next album release, rather than borrowing and paying back." But just as he was accomplishing a sought-after goal, his personal life was pushing him away from music. Push and pull: music and environmentalism, music and family. In the following months, he would have to work out his ambivalence about his career, one more time.

A nova is a star that ejects some of its material in the form of a cloud and becomes more luminous in the process. Nova Minowa was born in October 2009. Eleven months later, Cloud Cult released *Light Chasers,* and a favorite on this album is "You Were Born," a quiet, beautiful song in which Minowa celebrates this new son, sometimes in surprising lines ("Love your mother, yeah she's a good one / She'll build you armor, keep you warm as a hen"), sometimes in direct outpourings of love. Playing a simple acoustic guitar melody line, accompanied sparingly by piano and violin, he sings to his son, who he calls his "precious" and his "love": "I don't know where we come from, and I don't know where we go / But my arms were made to hold you, so I will never let you go / 'Cause you were born, to change this life." The song is emotional, and while pop songs about love are almost always directed toward romantic, sexual feelings between two grown people, Minowa applies the language of the pop song to his literal baby, challenging our notion of what it means to hold one's love in one's arms.

The year was full of change for the Minowas. After becoming a father, Craig realized that he couldn't continue his work in environmental science for the Organic Consumers Association; he moved full-time into the music business, scoring nature documentaries for National Geographic as well as writing Cloud Cult songs for the next album. Reviving their plans to turn Earthology Records into Earthology Institute, a nonprofit sustainability learning center, the Minowas moved when Connie was eight months pregnant from their old farmhouse in northern Minnesota to a new place in Viroqua, Wisconsin, a beautiful midwestern landscape known as the driftless region, home to the farming cooperative Organic Valley as well as to numerous like-minded people.

When Cloud Cult ended its tour the previous summer, band members weren't sure what the future would hold for the group. An announcement from Minowa several months later that the band would be holding auditions for a multi-instrumentalist, someone to play keyboards and another instrument, suggested that the band would continue. After extensive interviews and auditions, Cloud Cult hired Sarah Elhardt (now Elhardt-Perbix), a pianist and vocalist who also plays trumpet and French horn. In typical Cloud Cult fashion, Elhardt got thrown right in. "I went to my first rehearsal with the band," she recalls, "as they were prepping for a First Ave show the next night. There was too much material to possibly nail down in one rehearsal so I was able to go to the show and experience Cloud Cult in the crowd. I was completely blown away and cried through most of the set. The next day I was talking with Sarah Young and telling her how amazing it was, and after a long pause she invited me to come along on their college show at Grinnell and play."

In April Cloud Cult performed in Chicago, in Madison, Wisconsin, and at the University of Minnesota for Earth Day. On that day, April 20, *PBS Newshour* ran an Art Beat article, "Two Companies Make It Easy Being Green," which praised Reverb and Earthology Records for their environmental efforts in the music industry. Also on April 20, Cloud Cult released a four-song EP, which included the album's new single "Running with the Wolves," which immediately got major airtime at independent radio stations across the country. In June and July Cloud Cult played festival gigs throughout the Midwest. And on September 14, 2010, it released *Light Chasers,* a transcendent art-rock, orchestral pop album, a fifty-six-minute concept record that Minowa says is "structured like a book."

In an interview with Skip Daly in *Guitar International,* Minowa talks about why he wanted to make a concept album: "A lot of music critics have claimed the album is dead. Most people listen to one or two songs off an album or listen to a random mix of songs on their iPods. I think that's great, but I also think there's something to be said about the full album experience. . . . I really believe in the album as an over-all piece of art. . . . Our most popular music has gotten to the point of being three-minute songs that go into random shuffle on an iPod. I think that there's so much more that a listener can get if they're spending an hour with a piece of work that's deliberately put together as one solid piece." To Annamarya Scaccia in *Blurt Online,* he explained more: "I just really personally enjoy the amount of artistic space a full hour of music can give you. It lets me take one central concept that is key in my life and spend a couple of years really trying to figure it out. I like the process of trying to see how all the songs play with each other into one large piece. I think it's probably the classical background I have."

Of all the Cloud Cult albums, *Light Chasers* sounds the most orchestral, perhaps in part because Minowa was now writing to a large extent for his enlarged band; the addition of Elhardt-Perbix meant he had more brass and keyboards possible for concerts. But the album is decidedly in the Cloud Cult vernacular. Hearkening back to *Aurora Borealis* and the cosmic philosophizing there, we have the framework of the epic starship journey. Hearkening to *The Meaning of 8,* we have religious rituals that serve as unifying motifs. Hearkening to *They Live on the Sun* and *Advice from the Happy Hippopotamus* (really, all the albums), we have a personal story of hardship and forward movement, and the personal psychology that must be dealt with and transformed.

Unlike *The Meaning of 8,* which announces its ambitions in the liner notes and matches songs to an explanatory philosophy, *Light Chasers'* themes and concepts are implicit and contextual, there to be dug out by the serious listener. The album's structure is like a symphony broken into songs, or an epic novel broken into connected short stories. In popular music, *Light Chasers* could be compared to concept albums by Pink Floyd, Bruce Springsteen, and Radiohead, albums where the parts are understood by a general grasping of the whole, which comes because of better understanding of the parts (the songs), which leads to reinterpretation, in a continuing cycle. The album is complex enough that with every new play you see or hear lyrical or sonic relations you hadn't noticed before.

In his poem "Auguries of Innocence," William Blake penned the lines that have since become famous as a metaphor for extolling how the human mind can comprehend design in the universe.

Blake urges humans "to see a world in a grain of sand / And a heaven in a wildflower," and the theme of *Light Chasers* is nothing less than how humans can create their own understanding of the world by seeing the resemblances between an individual life and human history, between philosophy of previous centuries and folk wisdom of today. The universe coheres in spectacular fashion because we are all living things, have all developed slowly over time to be in tune with one another, and the human imagination uses its creative powers to understand this in ways big and small. But, Minowa would caution here, many of us have trouble contemplating the grand or the small, have trouble going beyond the everyday matters of our own lives.

Light Chasers is an ambitious album, and perhaps the best comparisons are to works in other genres, such as the film *2001: A Space Odyssey* or even James Joyce's novel *Ulysses*. Each song has a title and a descriptive category, such as the first song, "The Mission: Unexplainable Stories," which is followed by "The Departure: Today We Give Ourselves to the Fire." Five of the songs, some of which are short and serve mainly as connecting musical transitions, are subtitled "Journey to the Light," and the album closes with the rousing "The Arrival: There's So Much Energy in Us." The space journey motif, embedded into the album's sound of rich orchestral arrangements layered into rock beats and striking melodies, makes the record seem like a long thematic symphony or a soundtrack for a National Geographic special on the cosmos.

The album opens with a French horn solo underscored with trombone lines—in mood, a sound reminiscent of Richard Strauss's *Also sprach Zarathustra*. Expressive drumming and beautiful violin and cello parts join the horns, and the entire sound gives a sense of someone or something gliding along in the atmosphere, perfect music for a ride in a hot air balloon. The lyrics begin: "We've been searching for our whole life / We have traveled through unexplainable stories." If you know the Minowas' history, then you know the autobiographical kernel. What they've come through and survived was probably unimaginable to them eight years earlier. But this song can also serve as just a general opening to a concept album, launching literally and metaphorically the sense of traveling.

Light Chasers is a religious service in the metaphor of a space journey. After announcing the traveling theme in the first song, the next, the hard-driving rocker "Today We Give Ourselves to the Fire," introduces the need to be purified, to enter into a consecrated endeavor. "Put out your hands," the leader says, "I know you're scared." The band members all together follow with "Light up your fire / Light up your fire / I know it's scary." At the two-minute mark, when instrumentals take over, the music sounds like the group has been launched into space.

"You'll Be Bright: Invocation Part 1" follows, a song that continues the religious structure by serving as a form of prayer that people hear at the beginning of a religious service or public ceremony. In context, this brilliant rocking song is both a petitioning or supplication for help, and the act of calling upon a divine being by incantation. One measure of this album's artistic strength is that any song, almost any set of lines, can simultaneously describe Minowa's life, humanity's attempt to make meaning out of life through ritual, and the exploration of far-off galaxies as a way to know where earthlings exist in a larger system. Does one find at the end of that journey a divine being or the potential divinity in humans? Either, depending on your beliefs. What, both physical and spiritual, is part of this journey? Certainly birth and love, as "The Birth: Journey to the Light Part 2" is followed by the song about Connie and Craig's new baby, "You Were Born." And whether the scale is small or large, about a particular human or all of humanity, Minowa links themes by using patterns of images.

"You were born to chase this light," he sings, and *light* and *bright* repeatedly relate metaphorically to an individual's spirituality.

The album shifts subtly with the middle set of songs, which together show the problems of human life. "The Lessons: Exploding People" suggests what happens when a person keeps things in and pursues a materialistic life: "You never see the present 'cause you're always looking back / Counting down the seconds to a heart attack," or "Bottle it up, and the bottle goes crack." The end result? "One by one the people they explode." In the psychological critique "The Battle: Room Full of People in Your Head," Minowa further elucidates his view of why humans lead such lives. The singer splits his character into various parts (Ego, Self-Pity, The Hangman looking for a scapegoat, The Victim, and so forth), singing "I've got each of these in me." This heavily symbolic song not only suggests that we adopt roles and then act out certain behaviors appropriate to those roles, but argues that we must acknowledge these roles and deal with them better. Within the album's mythic frameworks, these songs and the ones that follow show how a human life, the human mind, and even a single day are alike, versions of the same structure.

A concert favorite and independent radio station single, "The Escape: Running with the Wolves" is a Thoreauvian declaration of independence; the song has a lighter sound, lighter vocal, and a terrific guitar riff reminiscent of U2's Edge. "The Acceptance: Responsible" is the stage after "the escape"; a simple piano opening consisting of chords and a few fills is followed by Minowa singing, "If for just a moment, you had to be responsible / For all the things you've said and done / Would you sit back and relax, or fasten all your safety belts?" To contemplate how to lead a good life, the song suggests, you gather yourself and accept responsibility for how your life has gone. In religious terms, this would be a moment of quietude and acceptance, of humility before a greater power, which here is simply Human Life. From such "Acceptance" comes recognition of "The Strength: Forces of the Unseen," one of the album's many memorable songs. The images of *light* and *bright* are joined by *energy* and the earlier *fire*—all come together in an assertion by the speaker that he can get through difficult times, whether events in his life or his own human problems. "We have so much energy that you can't see," he sings, and praises the humble power that comes from "the warmth when you're next to me, the bright white light of the fevered dream, the roots of the tree"—all the "forces of the unseen."

"Forces of the Unseen" serves as a climax to the album's themes, and the last three songs recapitulate and then close those themes. "Blessings: Invocation Part 2" begins with Alcoholics Anonymous sayings, Buddhist mantras, and chanting of mystic sects: "the wind's gonna blow where the wind's gonna blow," or "let come what may come and let go of what goes." A great guitar line overlays this chanting, with drumbeats and hand claps evoking an image of people in robes beginning some ritualistic service with drumming. Then Minowa sings over the top of this drumming, "Bless the children, safe sleeping / Don't leave me, don't leave me / Bless the parents, hearts aching," and so forth. Everything and everyone is told to travel safely (an echo of "You'll Be Bright"), and then we return to the metaphor of light chasing. The music builds relentlessly toward the end, and for a "blessings" song it's pretty rocking and stands in contrast to the quiet sounds of "The Awakening: Dawn," which follows.

With "Dawn" the day has begun again, and in this beautiful song, the sound of water dripping and flowing merges with a simple acoustic guitar strum and Minowa's voice: "All our anxieties are in a box I mailed to Pluto / And I feel like the sun." A song of renewal, "The Awakening: Dawn" becomes a love song that becomes a further renewal:

We rest our heads upon one pillow.
Beg for falling stars to break in our window.
Outside the evergreens blow out their birthday candles,
I feel like the wind. Ooh, aah—Gonna blow it all away.

Pray to the "I Don't Know" that made me.
Protect my Love, protect my friends, protect my baby.
I have worries, but I'm not going crazy.
I feel like the rain. Ooh, aah—Gonna wash it all away.

I can't breathe unless you're in my air.
I'm not here unless you're somewhere near.
When old age calls, we'll share a rocking chair.
And I feel like the dawn. Ooh, aah—The light is getting
near.

Renewal and dawn can get one ready for another attempt, and the short interlude "The Contact: Journey to the Light Part 5" serves as a link to the finale, the magisterial "The Arrival: There's So Much Energy in Us." The music opens with shimmering sounds as if a spacecraft is getting ready for takeoff, and then a glockenspiel enters, and then just one piano note followed by a few chords. The orchestral motif, the sound that signifies the journeying, comes in, with the drums kicking it off, joined by strings, which increase the energy, which is followed by a beautiful violin melody. Minowa sings, "A million years it's been, since the search began / Still can't find it, still can't find it," and the journey begins. The "I" and the crew stand in for all of humanity throughout human history, as well as an individual; the "it" is purpose or faith or a divine being or the meaning of human life. The crew takes "the written words of our philosophers" and builds a fire; the crew takes "the church's veil" and builds a mighty sail. The voyage continues but can't reach a destination. In the closing stanza, Minowa sings, "I finally see it, I finally see it." But it's not like a sea voyager sighting land, or a spaceship seeing a new star; what we're close to, and what the goal may be, is simply the acknowledgment that "there's so much energy in us." We can search for wisdom and understanding and can lead good lives. Most of all, we can simply keep voyaging.

Critics were generally positive about the new record. Marc Hogan reviewed it for *Pitchfork* and called the album epic, millennial indie rock; and John Richards, the influential deejay at KEXP in Seattle, said that *Light Chasers* is "the best thing Cloud Cult has ever done, which is saying a lot as everything they've done so far is near perfection." Blogosphere chatter was equally strong. In a long review, "The Return of the Album: Cloud Cult's *Light Chasers,*" Tony Van Zeyl, who writes for the St. Louis online entertainment site Playback:stl, praised the album as his favorite of the year and also argued for Cloud Cult to be in the conversation about the great bands of our time.

To promote the record, the band did its usual college radio campaign, and not only did the album chart well on the *CMJ* charts, but *Light Chasers* was its first album to make the *Billboard* charts. The band was also more aggressive in promoting the record with videos for YouTube play. Band members decided to follow in the spirit of their performance art, hiring animators to merge art and music. They sent Jon Thompson, aka Munkabum, a prerelease copy of *Light Chasers* so he could pick out a track to animate, and he chose the opening song, "Unexplainable Stories." The band also approached animators they hadn't worked with before but whose work they admired. Eric Power, an animator/music video director from Austin, Texas, created a video for the first single,

"Running with the Wolves," and he appreciated the artistic free-dom he had to interpret the song: "I loved the energy of the song. . . . I wanted to capture the idea of returning to a more primal state and becoming more in touch with nature. The video shows this by gradually becoming more colorful and lush the farther the two characters get from civilization." Cloud Cult sent several songs to Dan Huiting, a filmmaker and senior producer of "City of Music" on Pitchfork.tv, and Huiting chose "You'll Be Bright." Cloud Cult would eventually take these videos on tour and show them on a big screen behind the band when it played the song, so that the concert had three visuals: the band's per-formance, Connie Minowa and Scott West at the back of the stage painting on their own canvases, and an animated video above and behind them.

The new songs became the focus of the concerts, not just because they are beautiful and really rock, but because the band could create a story within the concert that mirrored the album's narrative of journeying and arrival. Its national tour began at St. Olaf College in Minnesota in early September, then went west to Denver and Boulder, then north for gigs in Bozeman and Missoula, Montana. West Coast stops in Seattle, Portland, San Francisco, and Los Angeles followed, before the band headed east a month later to play Boston, Brooklyn, New York, Philadelphia, and Wash-ington, D.C., among other cities. They did interviews and in-studio sessions along the way, including a reappearance on the influen-tial *Soundcheck* on WNYC in late October and an excellent session with David Dye on *World Café*, a show originating from the NPR station out of Philadelphia. In November Cloud Cult headed home to Minneapolis.

For this tour, the band didn't have to scrimp on every ex-pense, and there was a general feeling of exuberance and ful-fillment. Sarah Elhardt-Perbix remembers the camaraderie: "I think that when I joined the band, the dynamics changed a bit. To add another girl to the mix created some sort of girl power thing that we reveled in. Sarah/Shannon/Sarah were the three S's that could not be stopped. It all started with one of the first nights where my competitive side stepped up and I wanted to race the boys. Straight up fifty-yard dash through the parking lot of the hotel—Shawn, Jeff, and I ready to put it all on the line. Our rooms were on the second floor with balconies overlooking the parking lot. That's where the girl cheers, chants, and taunts began. The boys had a cheer squad too but not half as loud as ours! I held my own, but Jeff still beat me in the end. From then on, the girls really hung together. It was so fun."

While ticket sales for this tour were strong in the usual markets (Seattle, Boston, New York, Chicago, Madison, Minneapolis), they were surprisingly weak in cities such as Portland and Philadelphia. Jeff Johnson, the tour manager, attributes the earlier climb to the band's novelty: "In 2007 and 2008, we were part of a 'scene,' we were an indie band that people thought they should go to hear. There was a lot of press about the band then." But if Cloud Cult had hit a plateau, it was a good place to be. Former band manager Adrian Young suggests that the fan base is more faithful in part because of the environmental and communal principles the band espouses and practices: "The people that are drawn to the band because of its ideals are loyal. It's nice to have a solid fan base that's extremely supportive, something that many bands these days don't have. Many fans just listen to music and consume what's new, spit it out, and move on to the next best thing."

The meanings beyond music that Cloud Cult taps into were exemplified by a concert on January 2, 2011, in Memphis, an unusually emotional affair even by Cloud Cult standards. Memphis is not a stop on a Cloud Cult tour, but the band was brought there by a prominent Tennessee businesswoman, Gayle Rose. Two years earlier Rose's nineteen-year-old son, Max, a student at Rhodes College in Memphis, had been killed in a car accident. Before his death, he was working at Streets Ministries, a Memphis organization pledged to helping impoverished youth; he was tutoring struggling students three nights a week in Hickory Hill, a predominantly African American neighborhood; and to his friends he was handing out CDs of his favorite band, Cloud Cult.

Max left behind a short legacy of service, his mom says, but one influential enough that his friends wanted to adopt it: "They were calling me individually, saying, 'Mrs. Rose, we want to serve like Max did. You know, what can we do to get involved?' That's when an idea hit me, what I now call vigilante philanthropy, where we could get a team, where we could go out and see where there's a need. In Memphis, that is every single day." Team Max was born and has thrived ever since, using Facebook to coordinate events. "We started to send out messages," says Rose. "You know, show up this weekend, we're going to do something for the Memphis Food Bank."

Organizing Team Max events is only the latest phase of Rose's humanitarian efforts in Memphis and elsewhere, and some of these have centered on music, a lifelong love of hers—she is a classically trained musician. When she discovered in Max's backpack numerous poems as well as *Feel Good Ghosts,* when she heard that he had been praising Cloud Cult for its music and principles, and then when she found out that Connie and Craig had lost Kaidin, Rose felt a profound connection. Coming to know their music and story, she flew to Denver to see the band perform there in September 2010, where she was moved deeply by the entire experience. She went home and wrote up a proposal for a Cloud Cult–Team Max benefit concert, proceeds going to buy bike helmets for inner-city Memphis kids to use on the Shelby Farms

Greenline, a seven-mile paved trail linking midtown Memphis to a large park. Two years after Max's death, at a memorial benefit concert that she had thought up and made happen, Rose saw Minowa walk onto the stage in a Team Max T-shirt. "I felt so much emotion," she recalls, "that I thought I was going to burst."

While the concert in Memphis was memorable for its importance to a grieving family and its direct community outreach, the Orchestra Hall concert in Minneapolis in July 2011 was a different kind of landmark, as Cloud Cult played to its largest ever nonfestival audience, an audience there just to see the band. In a venue with excellent acoustics, with an adoring hometown crowd that was quiet when the music needed to be heard and raucous in its appreciation, Cloud Cult was on fire from the opening chords. All the band members cite the concert as one of their all-time favorites, a high-water mark of energy and musicianship. Emotional highs such as the concerts in Memphis and Minneapolis help sustain a band, but just as crucial for a band's longevity is how members deal with difficulties and change.

Shortly after the Memphis concert in January 2011, the band canceled bookings because Minowa had developed a heart issue that made him weak and faint; one chamber of his heart was enlarged and not pumping blood well. The wait to be seen at the Mayo Clinic in Rochester, Minnesota, was lengthy, but a Cloud Cult fan heard about what was going on and knew the doctor there who did the specific kind of surgery needed. "I got an appointment in a few days instead of a few weeks," Minowa recalls. "I had heart ablation surgery, and I've felt great ever since. They then wondered if what was going on with my heart could be tied to why Kaidin passed away, since his death is still a mystery. There's a rare heart disease that could tie what happened to me with Kaidin's passing, but insurance wouldn't cover the tests to find that out. Another Cloud Cult fan heard about that and knew a doctor overseas who does the testing, and that doctor said they'd do the tests for free. It's not like we have a million fans out there, so it's incredibly amazing that in both of these cases, something strange and rare was happening to me, but these people came out of the woodwork to guide me through it. There are times in life where you can't help but feel like there's something bigger out there taking care of you."

A difficulty of another sort came shortly thereafter, when Cloud Cult needed to hire a new cellist to replace Sarah Young, who had been with Minowa going back to 1995. Fans had long noted Young's musical abilities and grace on stage, and other band members looked up to her for her kindness and generosity, admiring how she juggled playing in the band with taking care of her children and working as a hospital nurse when not on tour. But she was pregnant with her third child, and her first two were nearing school age, and it was time for the family to stay put. After a lengthy audition process for a new cellist, Daniel Zamzow was offered the position; he debuted with the band at St. Catherine University in St. Paul in April. Though 2011 began with difficulties, overcoming them showed the band could go on, and the end of the year brought a different kind of event that demonstrated life goes on: Iris Minowa was born in December.

Our culture, loving fame and fortune, idolizes celebrities and celebrity culture. We admire comeback stories, where a star athlete or promising politician hits bottom but then, through determination and desire, regains the top. We almost always, for public consumption, focus on pinnacle moments that can be measured: an Oscar, a championship. The Minowas are a comeback story, indeed, but what finally matters most in that story are not the pinnacles but simply the enduring that Craig and Connie underwent and the wisdom they achieved. In an interview that summer for *Guitar International,* Skip Daly asked Craig what he does for fun, and got a reply, said Daly, that "might be the best answer I ever got" to that question. "Play with my boy," said Craig, "Have family time. Take some time where we turn off the phones and turn off the computers, and nobody can access us. Spend time together, whatever it is . . . really it makes no difference, as long as we're spending time together. It just feels so incredibly nice. Hanging out with him and just watching him grow is probably the most relaxing and healing thing in my life right now. And, of course, being with my wife and having that nurturing and loving relationship . . . having the patience with learning how to go from the business of where you sit down at a computer and you have absolute control over what direction a song will go . . . versus going back to 'real life' where you never know what you're going to be handed. Having a loving family that's going through all that with you is an incredibly spiritual way to spend your time."

For most of its concerts on this tour, Cloud Cult closed with the final song of *Light Chasers,* "There's So Much Energy in Us." The song served well the concert's emotional arc. As a majestic song of journeying where a crew searches for an "it" that will explain ultimate meanings, "There's So Much Energy in Us" worked metaphorically in concert as the Cloud Cult story. Full of grandeur in its orchestral rock arrangement of strings, horns, guitars, keyboards, and drums, the song embodies the niche that Cloud Cult has come to inhabit: strange and gorgeous rock and roll, spiritual questing, optimism in the face of difficulty. If there's no straightforward answer given for how to find "it" (though "You're always close to it," the captain says near the end of the song), some suggestions from all its albums together tell us what to do: trust, love, be creative, believe, and search, by yourself and with others.

Fans Write

I can't think of another band that captures the true essence of freedom and hope quite like Cloud Cult. I clearly remember the music of Cloud Cult coming to me and restoring my hope at a moment of utter despair. My husband and I were in the throes of the adoption process. This journey involved cumbersome paperwork, painful waiting, and a lot of uncertainty. It also involved a trip to the rural countryside of Ethiopia to meet our child in an orphanage. After spending only a few short minutes with her, we had to leave her behind while the government processed paperwork. Meeting this perfect, beautiful little soul and then letting her go was one of the most difficult things I had ever had to do.

The evening after we met her, I checked my e-mail in a state of complete sorrow. I discovered that a friend had e-mailed me the lyrics to "You Were Born," hoping to encourage and lift me up on this difficult day. I sobbed, releasing my anxiety and pain as I sat before the glowing computer screen. I knew in that moment that our child was born for a reason, and that she would be in our arms, safe and sound. I read the words over and over, "The stars may fall, and the rain may pour, but I will love you evermore." No matter what happened with our paperwork, no matter how long it took to bring her to our family, I would love this child forever. In that moment, life became simple and I was set free. There is so much hope in a moment like this. It's a moment during which you realize that life's not about pushing paperwork in a cubicle or hoarding cash in fat bank accounts. It's about chasing the light and sharing the fire. Two months after this evening, my husband and I returned to Ethiopia, and our daughter joined our family forever. We still sing her to sleep with the song "You Were Born," and her favorite evening activity is to rock out and dance to other Cloud Cult tracks. She is safe and sound and chasing her own light in her darling three-year-old way.

—Rachel Jorgensen, 31, Ramsey, Minnesota

In 2010 I heard my first Cloud Cult song, "No One Said It Would Be Easy." I immediately bought the album. That same year I saw my first Cloud Cult show. I was in the front, and it was exhilarating. They opened with "Unexplainable Stories." In 2011 I was diagnosed with bipolar disorder, then a seizure disorder, and post-traumatic stress disorder and had to drop out of school. In 2012, after a long struggle in my head I was diagnosed with paranoid schizophrenia. There's truly a room full of people in my head. It makes life a constant struggle between my rational and irrational self. It's an unexplainable story.

I remember one cold morning standing out in my backyard listening to that song in my headphones and clinging to a cigarette, hands shaking, awaiting to be admitted to a mental hospital in just an hour. It gave me courage. I remember sitting in the woods one night in the face of all my anxiety and my delusions, blasting "Forces of the Unseen" in my headphones, mouthing along with the words "I'm gonna make it through, you'll see. / I swear I'll prove you wrong. / You haven't seen the last of me. / I am way too strong." In those moments you feel dead, you feel death, decay, the rotting forces of this earth, the things that plague the body and mind that no human deserves. Cloud Cult deals with that feeling by combating it with the idea of energy, which is just as natural as the decay it combats, but somehow overpowers. I see this energy when they play live, when they swirl their paint canvases, and when I hear Craig and Connie's story. Listening to Cloud Cult makes me believe that I must have at least a little bit of this energy inside of myself, and if so, the ability to rise above the demons inside me, the pain I feel, all the pills I take, and feel a transcendent goodness, if only for the length of a four-minute song.

—Michael Vickers, 20, Elmhurst, Illinois

Cloud Cult's music has been the soundtrack to my tragedies and my joys. I had three amazing daughters, and we would listen to Cloud Cult as a family almost daily. You can imagine how excited I was to be able to take them to see the band play live on May 4, 2012. The girls were blown away by the experience, especially my middle daughter, who was eight and a budding artist. Watching them feel the music with their whole bodies and the amazement spread across their faces as the paintings took shape will always be one of the most precious memories I have. I looked forward to taking them to many more concerts, but unfortunately that was the last concert they would ever attend.

On July 10 my daughters were ripped from this world, and the beautiful music that Cloud Cult has created over the years took on a whole new meaning for me. It was like I discovered that a pond I thought was six feet deep was actually a thousand feet. I was trying to put together a song list for the memorial ser-vice and found myself on the band's web page when I sent them an e-mail thanking them for the gift of their music and what it meant to my girls. The band responded to me with so much love and caring. They came to the memorial and played live for my girls one last time.

Their music gives voice to my grief and eases my constant

pain with hope and understanding. Cloud Cult's songs continue to help me pull through each day, and I can sincerely say that I would not have made it without their music.

—Jessica Schaffhausen, 32, River Falls, Wisconsin

I knew we were the only people in the house, but it felt more like we were the only people in the world. Just my daughter, Natali, son, Bryson, girlfriend Ashley, and myself, preparing dinner in the kitchen. The Hamburger Helper was on the stove, the green bean casserole in the oven, and my favorite band Cloud Cult was playing on the stereo. Looking outside I could see nothing but darkness, while the kitchen inside was full of a bright radiance.

I'm standing in the dimly lit dining room holding Bryson when the song "Journey of the Featherless" comes on. I hug my son tight and begin dancing across the floor. He smiles and laughs as we jump and spin. Ashley and Natali instantly follow, holding hands and dancing in circles. We all join together in the kitchen, dancing back and forth in a circle of pure happiness. The song comes to an end and with it our dancing. The children run into the living room while I stay next to Ashley. We turn to each other to see that we both have the most genuine of smiles and eyes filled with tears of joy. We slowly embrace each other, and I think to myself, "I have never loved you more in my entire life."

Cloud Cult is about making sure to live life filled with happiness and love, no matter how hard it can be or seem.

—Zack Bennett, 27, Midland, Michigan

I unfortunately can't remember who suggested Cloud Cult to me for the first time, but I ended up listening to the entirety of *Light Chasers* three times in a row. And then I ignored the rest of the songs and listened to "Room Full of People in Your Head" for another hour or two. The song encapsulates something fundamental about human nature and the way we process ourselves and the world around us. It's hard to make sure that the room is quiet and that everyone works together, but I always find it easier to be me after listening to this song. I really have all of these in me, and I suspect everyone else does. And I might not have ever understood this simple yet stunning truth without the contribution of Cloud Cult.

—Andrei Dumitrescu, 29, Bucharest, Romania

In the fall of 2010, I was creating a video to be used at the annual father–daughter dance at my daughter's high school. It was a video with pictures of all the senior girls and their dads when the girls were little and then as seventeen-year-olds. Among the songs I selected for background music was Cloud Cult's "You Were Born."

The photos were in alphabetical order. I added the songs and began editing in iMovie. The father of one of the girls died nine months before the dance. Her mom submitted the photos of Ellie and her dad, John. As their photos appeared in the show, the lyrics "Oh my precious, oh my love, when they come to take me I will hold you from above" played. (I am getting all teary just writing this, even two years later.)

They say that there are "thin places" where the barrier between this world and the next is more transparent. I believe that it was very thin that day and John McDonald reached through.

—Jennifer Summers Arriola, 49, Eagan, Minnesota

I first heard Cloud Cult when I was a sophomore in college, and I immediately fell in love with their raw sound and insightful lyrics. It was refreshing to hear music that was not about romantic heartbreak or desire but about the love between friends, family, and even strangers. As an environmentalist, I especially enjoy Cloud Cult's philosophies on how everything is connected, how we return to the earth, and how we are all, in the end, just made of water.

It is amazing that a band can cater to the happy and the sad, the whole and incomplete, the lonely and loved. Cloud Cult's message is timeless; they are the anthem for the soul searcher in us all.

—Natalie Warren, 24, Minneapolis, Minnesota

By some stroke of luck, my husband and I discovered Cloud Cult through our local radio station shortly after the premature birth of our twins. Born at twenty-six weeks and weighing just over a pound each, our son and daughter faced considerable odds. That first song, "Journey of the Featherless," has stayed with us through the most difficult time in our lives.

Losing our son after just two weeks, we faced mourning the loss of his life while at the same time watching our daughter battle for hers, literally bracing ourselves for losing her too and daring to hope that we might not. Listening to Cloud Cult, a group who sings about this deeply personal loss, the loss of a child, feels like belonging to a special club or group therapy. This group, however, connects through amazing lyrics and beautifully creative music instead of simple words—words that don't adequately reflect both our sorrow and longing, but also our enormous gratitude.

The music puts melodies to our thoughts and cradles the deepest feelings of anger, fear, and love and has helped us move toward healing with a greater understanding of our treasures. Our daughter is almost five now. Our son's ashes are scattered in a sacred body of water and buried beneath a western red cedar that we visit regularly, inscribed with the words, "we give you back to the water from where we're all born."

—Neil and Margo Young, 39 and 35, Seattle, Washington

Cloud Cult isn't just a band really. They are a way to believe, a way to move, a way to live. Since I was fourteen, they've been engraved in my mind, a constant song being played. I remember the night I first heard Craig's voice; the song was "Love You All." It just made sense to me, a song so simple that hit me in a way no other song had. After that night I was obsessed: constantly asking people if they had ever heard of them, telling my friends that they just had to listen to the magic. Most of them never did, but I stuck by the band's side, making sure I had every song I could get and memorizing every word just so it would be there when the music wasn't. I even e-mailed them a poem I wrote, a petty little poem to say the least, but Craig responded. He told me that no one had ever written them a poem before, so it was "pretty darn beautiful"; he said that he would forward it to the band as he was sure it would inspire them. Now, I know it can't possibly be the best thing he's ever read, but I could feel the sincerity through the little black letters on the screen. He made me feel as if it had been the best thing in the world.

I read the response over and over until I had it memorized. I knew if I were to send a sappy poem to any other band, I would have gotten an automatic message sent back telling me something insincere, with no love and no truth. But not Cloud Cult. They are love and truth. They teach it, they sing it, they believe in it.

—Alexis Ament, 19, Waconia, Minnesota

I suppose Cloud Cult reminds me that I am alive. They lift me above the numb, day-to-day routine that distracts us all from the beauty and big picture of life. Their music accesses a part of me that, despite all my life's changing and maturing, has remained constant since I was a kid. It's an inner dialogue or feeling that comes out in quiet moments of happiness, during successful bouts of personal reflection, after an emotionally refreshing conversation, while thinking fondly of my mother, family, and friends. It comes out in my darkness, when, at seventeen, I had my heart broken by the first love of my life, and I broke down in the arms of my mother like an infant; I remember it, underlying my confusion and fear, as I watched my parents argue at the age of six; it was present when the family dog passed in our trembling arms. It's these moments when you are able to remove yourself from the immediacy of a situation to see a bigger picture.

I believe that that part of me is the truest version of my self—it often gets drowned out by insecurities, daily routines, social norms, and all the other factors, both internal and external, that limit humans from genuine expression. I find that as I grow older, this part of me is becoming more and more difficult to access. But Cloud Cult makes me feel like a kid again, not in the way of playground cruelty and immaturity, but in the way of innocence and wonder. I think that's one of the reasons why parenthood has such profoundly transforming effects on adults—they are reminded of what matters about living. At twenty-one, kids are far off for me; in the meantime, I'm glad Cloud Cult can serve as a reminder.

Growing up in Orange County, California, I felt that many of the adults I was surrounded by followed similar paths to financial success. Just a year away from graduation at a university, I sometimes feel like a horse with blinkers on—racing toward this form of adulthood. It's an adulthood I often fear. It seems lifeless. It's refreshing to think that as I sit here on the verge of diving into my own adulthood, surrounded by career fairs, GPA competition, fake smiles, and disingenuous handshakes, there's a forty-year-old living out in the middle of nowhere, somewhere in Minnesota (now Wisconsin) doing exactly what he wants to do, and it's working. He's a human being I check myself against. Someone that reminds me to wake up, to love, to give thanks, to shut up for a second and listen, to never lose my kid side, to take it in stride, to feel it all.

—Justin Brown, 21, Seattle, Washington

Over the years, I have referred to many different acts as "my favorite band," generally not settling on one in particular for more than a few months. That all changed when I was first exposed to the music and mind-set of Cloud Cult. They changed my entire concept of what it means to be a favorite band. Never before had I heard so many profoundly powerful, incredibly relevant, and emotionally real philosophies and experiences espoused by one person—and all packaged in the most lush and beautifully arranged rock music I'd ever heard. Craig Minowa has said so many things that I either desperately needed to hear, or thought I was alone in believing. His honest and candid explorations of the darker aspects of human existence are powerful medicine, and his unshakable positivity, even in the wake of the loss of his son, is a beacon of hope and inspiration. The music of Cloud Cult has been pivotal in my own emotional and spiritual development, and also strengthened my resolve to join Mr. Minowa in his goal of exposing people to a positive and spiritual message through music. Every word, note, and strange noise in Cloud Cult's pantheon of diversely styled (but always impeccably produced) music is pure perfection, and I can say without a hint of exaggeration that this band is one of the things I am most grateful for. I consider their presence in my life a true blessing.

—Andrew S. Lentz, 20, Hopkins, Minnesota

It's extremely difficult to express exactly what Cloud Cult means to me because they have touched my life in so many ways. I was first introduced to Cloud Cult in high school by my friend Max while we were driving from Knoxville to Memphis. A couple years later, Max passed away in a car accident. At Max's visitation, his family chose "Love You All" as one of the songs that was to be played. And although I have always maintained a healthy level of skepticism toward the supernatural, Max's spirit was undoubtedly alive in Craig's lyrics that night. Max was only the beginning of my close encounters with Cloud Cult's powerful ability to transcend space and time with its music. Every single day, we are inundated with images of fear and hate, and it is incredibly encouraging to know that a band like Cloud Cult exists. Cloud Cult is a constant, otherworldly force of compassion, understanding, healing, and love. To this day, when I introduce friends to Cloud Cult, I think of the wonderful gift Max gave to me years ago. "When it's my time to go, I want you to know, I love you all."

—Peter Travis, 22, Orlando, Florida

Growing up I didn't really like the music on the radio, and the Internet was just getting started, so I didn't have a way to explore my own likes, hell, I didn't even know what my likes really were. At best I just went for music that had a good beat and a decent melody, with the occasional anxiety teen rock song thrown in for good measure.

Years later I saw an Esurance commercial and loved the song they were using on the background. Eventually I was able to figure out it was Cloud Cult's "Lucky Today." It was a different, fun, unique sound. I was hooked. I skipped getting insurance and excitedly bought the whole album *Advice from the Happy Hippopotamus*. I popped it in, ready for track one, and was confused, even a bit miffed. The upbeat banjo and happy melody I was expecting was replaced with string instruments and distortion. I was disappointed but drawn in by the drumbeat. I kept listening and realized how different and original Cloud Cult was.

As I listened more and more, buying more albums, I found that pattern repeated. Some of their albums took me a second or third listen before I really started to understand and get into it. With that process though, realizing their unique style took a bit, I felt like Cloud Cult became my band. Not everyone would get it, but that's OK, because I felt like I did. Once I got *Light Chasers* I was completely hooked. It was the best album I ever heard. Beautiful songs paired with lyrics that caused me to daydream, got my blood flowing, and even made me think about starting a new life off the grid (listen to "Running with the Wolves" and you'll understand). Whenever I'm in crowded traffic with my iPod on shuffle and it lands on the opening horns of "Unexplainable Stories," I find myself taking a deep, relaxing breath. It carries me to four minutes of bliss.

My favorite song however has to be "You'll Be Bright (Invocation Part 1)." The lyrics are my favorite reminder about how much life is out there to live. There is both good and bad, but the experience is important in making you who you are. "You'll Be Bright" even changed how I say good-bye. All I say to my friends is "travel safely," but in my head I'm sending them a carpe diem push.

Cloud Cult's music is a great escape, inspiration, something that actually speaks to me, a push to try something new, and a reminder to not let life pass me by.

—Nathan Jackson, 27, La Crescenta, California

My sweet, darling, loving mother died in May 2010. I had just graduated college and was a month shy of twenty-five. I was at a complete loss. I'm not a religious person by any means, and it was a very dark time in my life. I honestly didn't think I could go on without her. When I couldn't find comfort anywhere else and didn't want to be here without her, listening to Cloud Cult became a solace. The messages I took from their songs were exactly what I needed. Their music taught me that her energy and love lived on, and I wasn't the only person out there who believed in that! It was such a comfort and relief. I then bought the rest of the Cloud Cult albums I didn't already have and gleaned powerful meaning and messages from them. I've always kept quote books, mostly for song lyrics that speak to me. I have one dedicated solely to Cloud Cult lyrics and often rewrite my favorite lines. Their words mean so much to me. In my darkest times of missing my mother I listen to Cloud Cult and feel so much more at peace. I know her love lives on. I can't even describe how much that means to me. I even got a little tattoo of the number eight to remind me about the connectedness of life and death and the universe. It reminds me that while she may not physically be here, I know my mother's love will live forever.

I miss my mother every single day. I also listen to Cloud Cult every day.

—Chandra Shaw, 27, Bozeman, Montana

Your Show Starts Now

It's late afternoon, and I'm sitting nearly alone in the Majestic Theater in Madison, Wisconsin, watching Cloud Cult band members bringing in their gear from their trailer, setting it up to ready for a sound check. In come amps, microphones, instruments, computers, soundboards, a projector and screen, spinning easels, an endless number of cords, and rolls of duct tape. Madison is the seventh stop on the band's national tour in support of *Love,* its new album. The tour began in early April with an unusual gig at an unusual venue, the Phenix Theatre in Concord, New Hampshire, where during an hour-long acoustic Cloud Cult set, the audience participated in Shakti flow yoga guided by Asa of Om Yoga. Meditative sound sculpture followed the set, and this unique event combining Minowa's music, Buddhist meditation, and yoga practice served as a benefit to raise money to assist eleven-year-old Taj Bethel in his battle with a rare liver cancer. From Concord, the band headed down the East Coast, visiting its usual stops—Boston, New York, Philadelphia, and Washington, D.C.—before it headed back west, playing tour dates through the heartland. Last night the band played Chicago's Lincoln Hall, tonight Madison. Band members will have a short break before playing two shows in Minneapolis at First Ave next weekend, and then they head off for a West Coast swing through Seattle, Portland, San Francisco, Los Angeles, and San Diego.

The tour's venues have been medium-sized clubs with capacities typically from five hundred to seven hundred people, and most shows have sold out ahead of time, and the audiences have liked the new songs. Band members have been excited to be back traveling together, renewing their musical and friendship ties. They spend much of their time sitting in a van driving from one city to another, but Shawn Neary says that being on the road "is like a traveling summer camp," a sentiment echoed by others. "We're often giddy with excitement to hang out with each other," Sarah Elhardt-Perbix says. A Cloud Cult tour, however, is not the glamorous stereotype perpetuated in films and television: no fancy hotels, stretch limos, roadies, or employees from the label taking care of the never-ending details. As I watch band members set up their gear, I'm reminded that they do all the work themselves, from scheduling to unloading.

Fans who go to concerts are often unaware of how difficult life is for members of most bands. Ed Droste, who fronts the successful indie band Grizzly Bear, says ruefully that although his fans usually think the band has made it, and they mean financially as well as critically, he's not going to quit his day job or ever think that he can buy a house, get good insurance, sock money away for retirement, or do any of the things that most successful people pursuing careers simply assume about their financial life. Being in an unsuccessful band leads to an obvious decision— you end the band. Being in a successful band such as Cloud Cult means that you could be the poster child for the "New Economy," that tag that has been used since 2008 to describe how millions of talented young people are scrounging together part-time jobs in order to pay the bills and their student loans.

Playing in a touring band complicates a life because your day job has to allow you to pick up and head out. Shannon Frid-Rubin, Cloud Cult's violinist, worked for a number of years at the front desk of MacPhail Center for Music in Minneapolis, and coworkers covered her hours when she toured. She now gives private music lessons, occasionally giving her students a week off or setting up a lesson with another teacher. Sarah Elhardt-Perbix prepared in college for a career in music administration, and after graduation, she worked for the Minnesota Orchestra, then managed at the famed Dakota Jazz Club in Minneapolis—jobs she no longer could do once she began playing with Cloud Cult. She's now teaching piano and making up the lessons for her students when she leaves for a tour. Shawn Neary's main job is at an independent bookstore. "The people at Magers & Quinn have been amazing," he says, "so understanding when I leave to go on tour." Neary could never have envisioned his present life when he was graduating from Luther College, where he majored in political science and played tuba in the college band. He began law school, a launching pad for a career, but now patches together the part-time jobs of band member and bookstore worker.

Why do these musicians stay in the band and live these rather difficult lives? Band members' answers, although individual in the details, are remarkably similar. "It's not the path I thought my life would take," Neary says, "but it's hard to wish for a lot more." His view is echoed by Frid-Rubin: "I just love the band and the music so much that I'm happy to have the complications that come when you don't have a nine-to-five job."

No band member discounts the pleasure that comes from playing music and entertaining people, but each also derives enormous satisfaction in being part of something larger than entertainment. Before a tour begins, Minowa often shares with them heartbreaking yet affirming e-mails he's received. The band members often interact with fans after the shows, which means hearing personal testimonials. They know that Cloud Cult's music is tapping into spiritual veins that can send fans into deep and sometimes dark places. Elhardt-Perbix says that playing in Cloud Cult "has an emotional load, and sometimes it can get to be too much, feeling every emotion of the audience. We're not doing this for fame or fortune, and sometimes it's extremely heavy." But if the music has a purpose to heal people, she goes on to say, "I feel honored by being part of Cloud Cult."

Band members feel part of a purposeful calling. "It's gratifying," Neary says, echoing Elhardt-Perbix, "to share in something that has so much meaning, that is so central and reinvigorating to people's lives. It's gratifying to be part of the beauty that Cloud Cult's music is making."

"To have the opportunity," Frid-Rubin says, "to help get Craig's message across by performing on stage, while possibly transforming someone's life or getting them through a hard day, is a true blessing."

Band members remark repeatedly that the music has shaped their own journeying. During a concert, Neary says, he is reacting as both a producer of the music and a listener responding. "I have my own responses to the lyrics as I hear them on stage, have my own strong emotions." He talks with great feeling about Cloud Cult songs that have shaped his character and become part of his life.

Frid-Rubin says that song lyrics have become ingrained in her mind, making her a better person: "Playing Craig's emotional music and singing his positive lyrics night after night on a tour is similar to repeating a mantra over and over. He is a teacher and in his own way a spiritual guide to me and so many other people."

If these comments seem bighearted and idealistic, it's because they are. Compared to most bands, Cloud Cult has stayed intact: the size of the band has grown, but few members have left, and its current incarnation has been together for several years now. The stability exists in part because Minowa is clearly in control—there are no power struggles that often emerge in bands that share songwriting and front-man responsibilities. That control extends also to hiring, and as Minowa has added band members, he has chosen not just for musical ability but for character. And he's chosen bighearted, idealistic people who are also fine musicians.

Take Daniel Zamzow, the latest addition. Zamzow has a variety of music and audio engagements. For the volunteer-based, community radio station KFAI, he produces concert recordings and documentaries for the show *MinneCulture,* with the mission of highlighting the cultural diversity of Minnesota; he also produces for KFAI live concert presentations and audio documentaries. Under the moniker Deep Sea, he engineers and produces recordings for independent clients. He has recently begun volunteering for ACME (Advocates for Community through Musical Excellence), a North Minneapolis project that works with underprivileged kids by giving music lessons and having after-school orchestra classes, among other things. "I work super hard—way more than forty hours a week—for not much money, but I'm blessed to be doing projects like these," he says. "The services I provide to the community give back in ways that money can't buy." Zamzow plays his cello with the local groups Liminal Phase, Alter Eagle, Deep Soul Deities, Improvestra, and Cherry Spoon Orchestra, as well as in his solo act intended for meditative environments like yoga classes. Added to all that, when it's time for a Cloud Cult tour, he's on the road. And why would he want to add being part of a touring band to an incredibly demanding work life? Cloud Cult, Zamzow says, "is not about ego," and the band fosters qualities he admires: "It's easy to be a good person when all the elements are in place—it's easy to be honest or true when that's happening back at you." In Cloud Cult, he says, "I can be my best self."

As the equipment for the night's show gets set up, I wander to the back of the venue, where I meet David Rubin, Shannon's husband, who is carefully laying out CDs, posters, and T-shirts on a long table. I learn that he ran the merchandise table last night in Chicago and will do so again here, continuing a long-standing Cloud Cult tradition that a spouse will end up working for the band in some capacity. Rubin graduated last year from Northwestern University's law school, and in a difficult job market for new lawyers he got a position in Minneapolis, and he and Shannon have recently moved into a house in a lovely neighborhood. As we chat, I discover quickly that this is not the yuppie that the career arc might suggest. Rubin is dressed in not-new jeans and a sweatshirt, and he is just as humble as Minowa and the band, and when Shannon wanders over with a cup of coffee for him, I find out that they are now running the Cloud Cult web store out of their basement, filling orders and mailing out merchandise. I can only laugh.

After upwards of two hours of work, the gear is set up, and Jeff Johnson begins doing his magic back at the soundboard, merging the Cloud Cult technology with the venue's system. The band plays a song, or part of one, and then waits patiently while Johnson makes adjustments. When the band plays, he wanders the theater, trying to get a sense of the sound in different places. Part of the sound check seems like rehearsal, as the band practices the songs from their new album. Tonight the band will be debuting "1×1×1," and Minowa makes them go through it twice. An hour rolls by, Johnson says that he's ready, and so the band heads up to the green room, the waiting room just offstage that's a private place for the band to relax before and after the show. Band members make small talk and sing some three-part harmonies on a Bill Withers song that they heard on today's road trip; I learn after a few minutes that they're now waiting to perform a meet and greet with the winners of a local record store's concert promotion. I also learn that the band, after finishing the load-out last night in Chicago and getting to bed about 3:00 a.m., awoke early to do an acoustic set at a record store in Chicago at 10:00 a.m., before driving to Madison and beginning the load-in at 3:30.

On tour their average workday is about sixteen hours, and after a show they've gotten up as early as 5:00 a.m., when they were leaving Boston and had to make the in-studio session at WNYC in Manhattan by midmorning. It exhausts me just to hear about life on tour, particularly for the Minowas, who have Nova and Iris with them. I'm likewise amazed that the band members are not zombies, that they're animated and fun. I ask Minowa how he pulls it all off. He laughs. "Energy drinks. Lots of them."

After dinner, the band members join up again in the green room. Some friends stop by, chat briefly, and then leave. Various band members wander out into the audience to listen to Jesse Marchant, their opening act. A few minutes after Marchant finishes his set, band members walk out to do the final onstage preparations, getting the technology ready, putting the instruments and microphones in place. The painters take out buckets of water, brushes, and paints. And the band heads back to the green room.

For the next few minutes, each band member begins to get himself or herself ready to perform. Zamzow begins focusing exercises. Peiffer stretches and bounces, simulating to mild laughter a boxer's prefight routine. West and Connie Minowa look at images, rehearsing in their minds how they'll begin their paintings when the lights go down and the music begins. Then the members all get in a circle, clap hands, and sing a short, rousing, and metaphorical rendition of "The Hokey Pokey": "Put your whole self in—whoo—and pull your whole self out." Johnson leaves to assume his responsibilities on the soundboard. Minowa paces in place. Band members focus as small talk quiets and then ends. They can hear the crowd yelling from the theater, and the band members, in the final moments of their preconcert ritual, just stand in a circle, being together in spirit. Then Minowa says "all right," and they head out the door to the stage.

Cloud Cult enlarges the possibilities of a rock band concert. At the back of the stage when the music opens, West and
Connie begin throwing paint on large spinning canvases. Minowa
sings into the main microphone and plays lead guitar but also
constantly bends over to program his computer in front of him for
ambient sounds or various loops. To one side Frid-Rubin, the violinist and background vocalist, stands next to the sitting Zamzow,
who plays cello and also sings harmonies. On the other side of
Minowa, Neary thumps his bass with energy and flair and likewise
sings harmony, unless he's pounding on a single drum or grabbing
his trombone to add a layer of horn. Next to him Elhardt-Perbix is
on keyboards so Minowa can concentrate on guitar; sometimes
she plays French horn or trumpet to enrich the orchestral sound.
Between the painters, at the back of the stage, Peiffer smiles his
way through both quieter rhythms on cymbals and snare and
thunderous pounding on the toms and bass. The painters also
sing harmony, and on some songs they move from canvas to
microphone and back. Art in the guise of controlled chaos, the
band's performance pleasures the eye as well as the ear.

Cloud Cult's stage show is not the version shared by postmodern artists, who believe strongly that self is a role inhabited
or created for only the moment, ready to be changed for a different desired effect, changed as easily as one changes an outfit
that "speaks" a particular selfhood. The exemplar of such a view
is Lady Gaga, who on stage performs brilliantly a set of roles with
her sexuality, musicianship, and theatricality. Cloud Cult stands in
stark contrast to the postmodern performance of multiple selves.
It's hard to imagine a more sincere person than Craig, and when
he talks about setting a sense of prayer at his concerts, or when
Connie says that she paints on stage largely "to focus on beauty
and to convey an energy of love," we're far away from the hedo-
nistic territory of most rock shows. Cloud Cult merges its music,
backstory, and performance into a seamless whole. What they say

and how they act demonstrates humility, a trait necessary to create the feeling of ritual they want their concerts to exemplify.

The band opens this Madison show with a short instrumental from *Love,* moves into one of their old songs, "Chain Reaction," and then follows with a rousing "Running with the Wolves." The crowd sings along and cheers wildly between songs—the band has a strong following in Madison. "There's so much freakin' energy in here tonight," Minowa yells, and that energy never wanes as the band moves through its set list. The show is simply great, as the band melds most of *Love* with a few older pieces and many of its best songs from *Light Chasers.*

After the show ends, the crowd slowly files out, with many people just hanging around, lingering in the magic of the past two hours. The theater staff wants to clean, and they push the crowd eventually to the back, to the merchandise table, where the auction for the paintings has begun. Cloud Cult brings an audience to the artists, and the artists contribute to the experience of a Cloud Cult show, and this arrangement suits everyone. It's challenging for West and Connie to complete a painting so quickly—if there's something they don't like, they can't go back and begin again or fix it—and yet they feel that the constraints of the show have positively influenced their art. West sees parallels between music and painting, in rhythm and composition, in subject and mood: "I relate painting so much to music. I really see brush strokes as rhythm and the hue of the paint as a key signature, whether it's a major or minor—there is an emotion you react to with color the same way with a key signature." Mentioning that Cloud Cult has sped up her goals as an artist, Connie says that her studio work varies from abstract to impressionistic to very symbolic, but live painting allows for more play. "I have come to realize," she says about painting for Cloud Cult, "that I don't have to fit into a specific box that the art world may say I need to fit in to. I've learned that I don't have to mark my success by being in a museum. I can

be successful simply by someone being touched by a painting."
The last I look at the auction sheets, the bids for each painting
are over $800.

At the merchandise table, Frid-Rubin and Elhardt-Perbix
have arrived to help David Rubin sell CDs and T-shirts. They talk
to concertgoers, who seem mostly interested in sharing how
much they loved the show. Peiffer, who I think of as a bit shy and
reserved, talks animatedly to one person after another, signing
posters and promotional flyers, asking people their names, being
a great ambassador for the band. And onstage, Minowa and the
rest of the band members have begun the arduous process of
load-out: taking down the equipment, packing things up, carrying
gear to the trailer. It's well after midnight.

Pop music's quintessential subject is love: how we fall into and
out of it, how it transforms us, what we'll do to have it, how
sometimes we push it away even when we feel it. Fears and fantasies, sorrows and ecstasies—love feeds the strongest emotions. Though a million pop songs have been written about love,
listeners never have enough no matter the repetition of theme
and sentiment. "Some people want to fill the world with silly love
songs," sang Paul McCartney in a romantic, not silly, love song
that reached number one on the *Billboard* charts. On March 5,
2013, Cloud Cult released its new album *Love,* surprising fans
that this band would be jumping into this pop music subject. Moving 8,266 units in its first week, the album debuted at number
fifty-seven on the *Billboard* Top 200 albums chart, making it by
far the biggest first-week seller in Cloud Cult's history.

While the songs are nominally about love, Minowa consid-
ers a range of experiences that challenges our usual consider-
ations of love and the pop song. No song on the album has the
common narrative of "we met, fell headlong for one another, broke

up, and now my heart's shattered." No song remotely resembles something like Adele's iconic "Someone Like You." The only conventional love song here is the catchy "Meet Me Where You're Going," where in an upbeat, acoustic guitar-banjo-violin Americana sound, as if the Lumineers were cowriting and singing with Gillian Welch, the lyric attests to the singer's devotion as well as his deepening love: "Every day with you I say 'I do' / And it means so much more each time." At the center of Cloud Cult's *Love,* surrounded by two instrumentals that make it stand out even more, is "The Calling," a song about vocation. "There's so much more you're made to be," Minowa sings in a rock song with driving guitar and emphatic drums. "Scream it from the top of your lungs / You have a calling." Culturally we use *calling* to describe work that has a social or spiritual purpose, when career seems inappropriate: religious leaders are "called" to a congregation; someone leading a nonprofit organization might say she has a calling to do social justice work. But what does a calling have to do with love?

In an interview on NPR's *Morning Edition,* Minowa said that the album is about how we might allow love, rather than our wounds, to speak for our lives. The comment does not mean that wounds and hard times aren't present. Anyone knowing his story gets that. But he is trying to persuade us that love comes when we can give up a viewpoint that emphasizes only hardship, as he says in "You're the Only Thing in Your Way," the album's opening song:

> Fly, baby fly, until nothing can get you down
> Sing, baby sing, until it all comes out
> You are the wind, the flood, and the flame
> Nothing here can get in your way
> You've come too far to care what they say
> Now you're the only thing in your way.

The album *Love* is actually about daily living, about spiritual matters, about relationships of all kinds—or, to be more precise, the album is about how to live daily in a spiritual way, in right relationship to the world.

Minowa showed in *The Meaning of 8* his personal journeying down the mystical path, and without announcing it as such, he shows in *Love* the end of that path. Mystics from all religions talk about love as the meaning of the universe. As in the album, such love isn't focused on a romantic relationship between two adults. The "peace that passeth understanding" is love. Mystics view life as interdependent and love as the glue that holds all things together. "Wisdom says I am nothing," says Sri Nisargadatta Maharaj, a Hindu mystic. "Love says that I am everything. Between the two my life moves."

Most of us live thinking primarily about our personal, narrow circumstances connected with our desires, the terrain of a pop song. To find our true deep beings, as well as a calling for our lives, we must look outwards to the world, recognizing that we are part of a nearly infinite series of interlocking, entangling webs. The comparative mythologist Joseph Campbell, borrowing from Buddhism, once said that humans should "participate joyfully in the sorrows of life." By acknowledging the pain and suffering of all life, human and nonhuman, a person can embrace living with less fear and anxiety and more clarity and affirmation—that is, with more love. As Minowa says in "Complicated Creation," "Gotta feel it, feel it all, feel it, feel it all / There's your medication." Or as he says in the beautiful song "It Takes a Lot":

> It takes a lot of broken heart
> To wonder why we get what we've got.
> But we get what we've got
> And when it comes to heart, my friend
> You've got a lot.

If a calling is work that we do with a whole, committed heart, the album's songs suggest we should approach love and life in that same way. "Where is your passion? Where is your wonder? Where is your thankfulness?" Minowa asks in "Sleepwalker." The songs almost always approach the topic from the viewpoint of the doer, the actor. The focus isn't on the object of love, but the one doing the loving and how that affects his or her life. Following "You're the Only Thing in Your Way," the album's second song, "It's Your Decision," reiterates personal agency while acknowledging the anger that can emerge as we go deeper into our own psyches. "Leave me alone," the speaker implores, "I'm going inward / I've got work to do disarming land mines / If I hold it in, I'll just blow up again." The sentiments here are not far removed from good self-help books ("Are you an angry one, or a feather? / Will you sink today, or let it float away? / It's your decision"), but what makes such lines more interesting of course is that they exist in an emotion accompanied or even created by the music. The sounds here mirror the sinking/floating, angry/light dichotomies: beautiful violin and cello duets augmented by acoustic guitar contrast strongly with intense, eerie electric guitar riffs and drumbeats, all accented with Muse-like piano arpeggios.

While the songs on *Love* are thematically tied, they do not blend in sound to create a concept album such as *Light Chasers.* The range of sound is wide, from the sweet, light, and melodic "Meet Me Where You're Going" and "You're the Only Thing in Your Way" to the distorted, ominous, heavy guitar strums and solos in "1×1×1," "The Calling," and "Sleepwalker." Three instrumentals give extended breaks to the word-heavy songs, almost like the long instrumental stretches that Modest Mouse and Death Cab for Cutie employ within songs. The songs on *Love* feel independent, as songs simply in their own right. Violin and cello lines, for example, appear more in duet with each other rather than as layers in music that sounds like an orchestral score. Several songs, such as

"Complicated Creation" and "Good Friend," hearken back to the playfulness, even goofiness, of early albums. We get hand claps, yelps and laughter, sustained shouting, spontaneous utterances, a bouncy rhythm section, and funny lines that are also serious:

> You know you are as small as the things you let annoy
> you
> And you know you are gigantic as the things that you
> adore.
> Some days you give thanks. Some days you give the
> finger.
> It's a complicated creation.

The songs from *Love* say, over and over, that we must quit moving through our lives on cruise control, must quit living life unaware. And what do we get when this happens, when we've learned the lesson to embrace things from a position of personal responsibility and love? We find good friends ("Good Friend"), we know how to create home ("Meet Me Where You're Going"), we find joy and empathy ("Sleepwalker"), we learn the "art of letting go" ("It Takes a Lot"). And when we've learned such lessons and know to live our life with purpose, what do we do next? A suggested answer comes in the powerful and moving "The Show Starts Now," a title and theme suited for an album's opening song, but the song that closes here.

"The Show Starts Now" begins with a two-beat "da dum," followed by noise sounding like a spacecraft orbiting. The piano enters playing two notes and holding the second in a descending line. To this spare, somber backdrop, Minowa begins singing, absorbing to his subject physics and mysticism, his grandma and chaos theory, all overlaid with Buddhist principles—two signature verses that could be written by no one other than Craig Minowa:

The physicist and the mystic say there's no such thing
   as time.
If God is now and everywhere, why's It so hard to find?
I wanna be the guy who lives in the moment, not so lost
   in my mind.
So I guess my show starts now. My show starts now.

Grandma said it don't matter, where we go to or come
   from.
She said, "Worry about what you're made to do, not
   what you're made of."
They say we're made of chaos. I say we're made of love.
And that means our show starts now. Our show starts
   now.

The first verse has "my show starts now," and the second "our show." When the third moves to "your show starts now," Minowa brings in a children's choir to sing the vocal, as if enlarging the message, particularly to the young. "Hold your breath for a better day / And you'll never learn how to breathe," they sing, and the album closes by urging us to live light, to breathe deeply, to love the world and trust that it will love back.

In "The Show Starts Now," Minowa sings the line that might serve as the current philosophical centerpiece of his journey: "I wanna be the guy who lives in the moment, not so lost in my mind." The first single from *Love*, "1×1×1," is a manifesto about how we might learn to be immediately present: "You are here to let the cards fall one by one / You're here to let your walls down one by one / You're here to peel the layers off one by one by one by one by one by one by one." The song is not pretty, filled as it is with distorted and ominous lead guitar lines. Don't try, Minowa sings, "to fill your holes with the next best thing," because the next best thing simply gives you more and more holes. Take your medicine, confront yourself honestly, and, the band sings-yells, "Peel your layers off one by one by one."

Most of us, as we move through the decades, add layers of protection: more stuff, more responsibilities, a career, a family, various images we have of our youthful selves. We make a life of accumulation, like a sea nautilus that adds new and larger chambers as it grows. Minowa is seeking in his personal relationships and art to peel his layers of self to get at bedrock, the essential self. He wants to live an exposed life, which is rather scary for any of us and all the more difficult for someone in the public eye. He exemplifies living a life without the protective belief that we can't influence anyone really but ourselves, a belief all the stronger when it's accompanied by the armor of irony.

On February 24, 2013, Stephen Thompson wrote a piece on *Love* for NPR's *First Listen,* where site visitors can listen free to all the songs two weeks before an album's release. Saying that Cloud Cult is the least ironic and cynical band in existence, Thompson praises *Love*'s emphasis on how humans must connect to each other and embrace the world, noting that true to form for the band, "the music that surrounds those messages bursts with warmth, whether in spare examinations of faith or in bighearted explosions of ecstatic celebration."

Virginia Prescott, host of *Word of Mouth,* a New Hampshire Public Radio show, also commented in an interview with Minowa that Cloud Cult is "just about the least cynical indie band I can think of." His response? "I think cynicism and just negativity in general has become all too fashionable. And we want to propagate something positive, because it is kind of contagious."

Prescott went on to ask about the band's desire to have

its tour be completely carbon neutral, and Minowa explained the various ways that they accomplish that, from how they make their CDs and T-shirts to the money spent planting trees (four times the suggested number because he believes that some trees die) and buying carbon offset credits from wind turbines. Hearing this, Prescott mentions wittily that Cloud Cult's efforts could be "a plotline from the show *Portlandia*. I mean, you're soooo good." After a brief laugh, Minowa replies with an idealism that simply demonstrates how spot-on is the *Portlandia* reference: "I think there's a really big responsibility when you're an artist with even somewhat of a modest following, and that responsibility is to try to use that limelight to propagate goodness. Whether we're artists in that literal form or artists of our lives, we've all got responsibility with our every day to try and make every moment be as good as possible." Minowa knows that his idealism and optimistic spirituality are an easy mark, but he seems not to care: "In what I create now, it's important to not be totally Pollyanna, and I want to have real human emotion and struggle in the albums. But there's a difference between using music as a method for whining about everything, and using music for confronting your problems with the intention of trying to figure out how to get better." People less idealistic than Minowa can admire, if nothing else, his courage to follow his principles.

In Charles Baxter's novel *The Feast of Love* (2001), the main character, Bradley Smith, has painted a magnificent canvas that draws everyone's attention. Unlike all the rest of his paintings, which are abstract and suggest destruction and a world gone wrong, this painting is full of color and light. *The Feast of Love* has food on a table in the foreground, but rather than recognizable dishes or drinks, a "visionary magic" abstracts the feast into blinding shapes of color. The narrator, Harry, observes that the table "seemed to be tipped toward the viewer, as if all this light, and all this food, and all this love, was about to slide into our laps. The feast of love was the feast of light, and it was about to become ours." But when Harry asks about the painting, Bradley explains that there are no humans in it because humans can't ever go there, can't ever feed at that feast. Married and unhappily divorced twice, Bradley tells Harry that the painting isn't true: "If you can't get there, then it's not true. . . . I don't spend my time painting foolish dreams and fantasies."

Perhaps because I've been teaching the novel this spring, I think of Bradley's painting often as I listen to Cloud Cult albums. If being divorced twice can embitter you, like Bradley, and make you believe that the feast of love is only a foolish dream, then having your adored young son die suddenly and without known cause could make you feel that the feast of life and love is certainly not for you. Countless people have suffered loss, and most of those have not succumbed to disabling grief, but we can still admire people such as Connie and Craig who have grieved deeply but then become ready to not only feast at that table of love but to make it for others. And this, finally, is the single most important story line for the Minowas: rather than be defined by tragedy, they have insisted on being defined by affirmation, on the energy that comes through the acts of journeying, performing, and loving.

In an earlier chapter, I discussed how albums over a period of time can be read as an autobiography: the self creates and performs the art, which shapes the self, which shapes the next artistic endeavor, and so forth in an endlessly recursive process. Exactly ten years passed between the releases of *They Live on the Sun* and *Love,* and the seven albums and numerous tours are testimony to perseverance and hard work. But an exemplary life and dedication to admirable principles are not enough to give a band a following—the fans have to love the music, of course, or they won't stay fans. And so the albums and tours are testimony

likewise to an art that shifted from dissonant outpourings springing from anger and sorrow to gorgeous chamber rock springing
from acceptance and love.

I began this project in part because I desired to comprehend how a song's message and art causes us to respond, to
make that song part of our own psychology or something we love
to sing along to. Scholars have certainly investigated widely what
effects music has on a hearer's mind and body, but no matter
how many studies scholars set up and how rigorously scientific
they make them, something always seems to be missing in the
explanations. I've read much about this subject, and ultimately I
can only say this: occasionally, when we listen to music, we are
a bell, and we're struck and we resonate our pleasure out to the
world. The human body and mind are mysterious, and when science solves some mysteries, others emerge, and what makes an
individual perceive deep beauty in music is one of those unsolved
mysteries.

For some music lovers, Pavarotti singing "Che Gelida
Manina" from *La Bohème* or an organist playing a Bach cantata
might be what thrills, what creates beauty somewhere in their
fibers. For fans of this band, it might be "Transistor Radio," "When
Water Comes to Life," "Everybody Here Is a Cloud," "There's So
Much Energy in Us," or "You Were Born." We often just don't know
why something rings us, but when any of these songs or any of
your favorites have rung you, just remember what one more great
Cloud Cult song has taught us: "Put out love, and they'll feel love /
It's a chain reaction." Our show starts now.

Acknowledgments

I could not have written this book without the cooperation of the band. Thank you to Craig and Connie Minowa, Sarah Elhardt-Perbix, Shannon Frid-Rubin, Shawn Neary, Arlen Peiffer, Scott West, and Daniel Zamzow. Thanks also to those who have been part of the band's journey through the years and who allowed me to interview them, particularly Jeff Johnson, Cody York, John Paul Burgess, and Adrian Young. Thanks to Craig's mother, Clarice Richardson, who with some trepidation allowed me to visit her. Craig Minowa gave me permission to quote song lyrics, and John Burgess gave me permission to quote from his documentary *No One Said It Would Be Easy*. Craig Minowa and Cody York provided the bulk of the photographs. The book is far richer for their generosity.

As identified in the book, numerous former bandmates, deejays at radio stations, people in the industry, music critics, and music bloggers responded generously to my e-mail questions and gave me insights. Others who talked with me and shared ideas about Cloud Cult's music include Natalie Warren, Alli Beardsley, Eve Adamson, Christian Graefe, and Chris Bowman. Thanks to Gayle Rose for sharing her story. I owe a great debt to two readers of the manuscript who gave feedback at early stages and helped me immensely: Zaq Baker and Marc Hogan. Much general thanks to all the people who want this book to succeed because they love Cloud Cult's music and wish the best for the band.

I could include only a small number of fan testimonials. To all of you who wrote, even if your words are not printed here, thank you very much. Your passion gave me hours of reading pleasure and moved me greatly.

Many thanks to all those at the University of Minnesota Press who turned the manuscript into this book, including my editor, Erik Anderson, himself a musician, who was an absolute delight to work with, and his editorial assistant, Kristian Tvedten, who shepherded the manuscript through the process. Mary Keirstead copyedited the manuscript and saved me from numerous errors.

I appreciate a sabbatical leave from St. Olaf College in the spring of 2013, during which I wrote portions of the book.

Parents are lucky to have influence reverse its direction. My children, Betsy Allister and Nat Allister, have helped me through the years become knowledgeable of bands that would likely have slipped by me unnoticed—what a joy to share music across generations. Most of all, thanks to my wife, Meredith Coole Allister, who listened to Cloud Cult music at home, attended concerts, read every chapter of the book in draft, never seemed to tire of my talk about the band, and encouraged me every step of the way.

Mark Allister is professor of English, environmental studies, and American studies at St. Olaf College in Northfield, Minnesota.

Mark Wheat is a host of 89.3 The Current on Minnesota Public Radio.

body and sun kisses from above as the clapping sounds of tambourines ring in the background and distant drums beat through your heart. I fell in love with that band from the first sounds of their "Pretty Voice"(s).

—Brandi Johns, 32, Baton Rouge, Louisiana

My husband and I have seen Cloud Cult so many times, over so many years. We meet someone and come away with a story, a memory, and are more in love with each other after every event. We truly believe Craig Minowa is a shaman. He conjures a fierce gamut of emotions in his followers with themes that are exceptionally intimate, yet universal and metaphoric, and are more powerful than years of therapy or organized religion. That he does this with such self-effacing humility and boyish astonishment is remarkable. To attend a Cloud Cult concert is to become part of something bigger than the sum of its parts, and I defy you to find another band who has such a respectful, good-natured, grateful, energized fan base. A Cloud Cult concert is a sing-along, a cry-along, a love-along.

We've followed their journey, we've followed them literally. We care about them, worry about them, are thrilled for them. My all-time favorite moment at a Cloud Cult show: at Lowertown (first local show since the birth of Nova), the previously reserved Connie spontaneously broke into dance, arms wide open and filled with joy. She's been dancing ever since.

In July 2011, we drove up from Minneapolis to see Cloud Cult at Bridgefest in Duluth. It was an unseasonably cold day. I repeatedly noticed a young woman, in a long, sleeveless black dress. She appeared to be alone, and she wandered the grounds as we did. She must be freezing, I thought. Eventually she added a T-shirt, purchased at the festival. Cloud Cult took the stage. I

Cloud Cult understood and accepted me when I was filled with self-hatred. "These are things that I keep hidden in my belly / I can't see them but they control my life." I opened up about my addictions. I got them in the light. I shed all that I was ashamed of. And found that people still liked me. They still accepted me. Even with all the horrible things I had done, they still loved me. I was still a good person in their eyes.

And through that love and acceptance and support I began to heal. To grow. To become who I am today. Spreading the love, compassion, and acceptance to others. Open yourself. Be brave. Forgive everyone everything. Heal. All because of a song.

—Dave Coleman, 40, Ontario, California

Cloud Cult came to me from my two college-age sons, Scott and Brandon. Like a gift from heaven, Cloud Cult's music became a common ground that has continued to bring us together over the years and been at the center of many thought-provoking conversations. When I saw them live for the first time, I sat in the back alone while my sons moved down to be front and center. I have never been more happy to be alone, to tear up when I needed to, to smile when I wanted to, to just "be" with the music. It was one of the most amazing live music experiences of my life. To this day, years later, whenever I listen to Cloud Cult, I literally feel my heart open up to every word, every sound, and to my own life. I'm not sure what else, if anything, in my life can invoke that response in me so flawlessly.

—Kathy Bigos, 51, Downington, Pennsylvania

Cloud Cult is the musical time warp that takes you to a field of daisies, lying in the cool grass with the wind softly caressing your